"In this book, Amy DiMarcangelo sets a lavish table for those of us who perpetually crave more. Her well-crafted content repeatedly points to God, the only one who satisfies our deepest longings. Having tasted what this world offers, are you still hungry? Read and feast."

Katie Faris, author, *He Will Be Enough: How God Takes You by the Hand Through Your Hardest Days*

"Encouraged, convicted, joyful, humbled, and full of hope. These are the things I experienced as I read *A Hunger for More*. To truly hunger for God and all he is can seem like such an overwhelming journey. But Amy so boldly draws us to the Father and his character, doing so with such beautiful compassion and truth. These words will be great encouragement to anyone who is longing for a hunger for God!"

Lauren Eberspacher, author, *From Blacktop to Dirt Road* and *Midnight Lullabies*

"This is a worship-inducing read. With both deep theology and winsome devotion, Amy lifts our gaze onto our wondrous and good God. *A Hunger for More* is a nourishing feast and a balm for weary readers."

Jen Oshman, author, *Enough about Me: Find Lasting Joy in the Age of Self*

"Who doesn't want to be satisfied? But so often, the things—even the good things—that we fill our lives with leave us empty. We crave something better. In *A Hunger for More*, Amy DiMarcangelo spreads a feast for women who have enjoyed plenty but have never had enough. With beautifully crafted sentences and biblical depth, DiMarcangelo serves readers course after course of only the best fare. In these pages, women can savor the richness of God himself. Are you hungry?"

Megan Hill, author, *Praying Together* and *A Place to Belong*; editor, The Gospel Coalition

"*A Hunger for More* invites us to stare down our desires and find our God sufficient to satisfy. Amy DiMarcangelo identifies—with wisdom and humility—the cravings that tempt our hearts, then entices us with the rich offerings found in our God. In each chapter her words serve to turn the diamond of the beauty of his character and promises. I found myself pausing my reading to stop and worship. *A Hunger for More* will confront your empty desires and offer the sweet satisfaction of being filled to all the fullness of God."

Jamie C. Finn, Executive Director, Foster the Family; author, *Foster the Family: Encouragement, Hope, and Practical Help for the Christian Foster Parent*

A Hunger for More

A Hunger for More

Finding Satisfaction in Jesus When
the Good Life Doesn't Fill You

Amy DiMarcangelo

WHEATON, ILLINOIS

A Hunger for More: Finding Satisfaction in Jesus When the Good Life Doesn't Fill You

Copyright © 2022 by Amy DiMarcangelo

Published by Crossway
        1300 Crescent Street
        Wheaton, Illinois 60187

Cover design: Lindy Martin

Cover image: Shutterstock

First printing 2022

Printed in the United States of America

Trade paperback ISBN: 978-1-4335-7510-5
ePub ISBN: 978-1-4335-7513-6
PDF ISBN: 978-1-4335-7511-2
Mobipocket ISBN: 978-1-4335-7512-9

Library of Congress Cataloging-in-Publication Data

Names: DiMarcangelo, Amy, 1988– author.
Title: A hunger for more : finding satisfaction in Jesus when the good life doesn't fill you / Amy DiMarcangelo.
Description: Wheaton, Illinois : Crossway, 2022. | Includes bibliographical references and index.
Identifiers: LCCN 2021042580 (print) | LCCN 2021042581 (ebook) | ISBN 9781433575105 (trade paperback) | ISBN 9781433575112 (pdf) | ISBN 9781433575129 (mobipocket) | ISBN 9781433575136 (epub)
Subjects: LCSH: Spirituality—Christianity. | Desire—Religious aspects—Christianity. | Contentment—Religious aspects—Christianity.
Classification: LCC BV4501.3 .D56 2022 (print) | LCC BV4501.3 (ebook) | DDC 248.4—dc23
LC record available at https://lccn.loc.gov/2021042580
LC ebook record available at https://lccn.loc.gov/2021042581

Crossway is a publishing ministry of Good News Publishers.

BP   31   30   29   28   27   26   25   24   23   22
15   14   13   12   11   10 9 8 7 6 5 4 3 2 1

To Mom and Dad,
thank you for teaching me of the surpassing worth of Christ.
Your hunger for God has profoundly impacted my own.

Contents

Introduction

I SAT AT THE RESTAURANT TABLE, pulled off my coat, and sighed in relief. I had just spent the afternoon hiking snow-covered trails with my sister and best friend. Even though we'd had such a good day, it left us exhausted and famished. We needed to be replenished—to rest our aching bodies and fill our empty bellies.

Our physical weariness that evening pointed to a universal truth: we are weak, needy, hungry beings. Sometimes we are oblivious to this reality; other times we are overwhelmed by it. Whether we realize it or not, we need to be filled. Caught up in day-to-day struggles, it is easy to forget the grace, hope, comfort, and strength given to us through the gospel. We may believe God's word is true, but in practice we don't always trust it. This disconnect between head and heart leaves us aching, no matter how "good" our lives appear.

I came to saving faith as a child. I don't remember exactly when, but I know I had a genuine awareness of my need for forgiveness and a love for the God who gives it. My story isn't one of rebellion or of going through the motions of religious duty while being spiritually dead inside. Despite temptations toward legalism, my obedience was predominantly motivated by love. I sinned in self-righteousness toward others but also confessed that failure and recognized my need to repent. I experienced seasons of spiritual dryness but undeniably drank from the well of living waters. There was plenty of sin in my life but no unconfessed skeletons in my closet. The same is true today.

Besides the spiritual blessings that accompany knowing Christ at a young age, my life has been filled with relational and material blessings as well. Raised in a loving Christian home, I have no stories to tell of abuse or neglect. I never endured any childhood trauma, unless you count the death of my guinea pig and the disappointment of being placed on the C team—the worst in the league—after missing soccer tryouts. Though adulthood has brought painful trials, I have experienced far more goodness than hardship. A loving marriage, three beautiful children, and a wonderful church are among the most precious gifts I enjoy. Despite all of this, I often ache for *more*.

I don't know your story. Maybe you're like me, and you grew up in a loving family and have walked with Christ for many years. Maybe your shelves are filled with well-worn books on theology, and you faithfully serve in your local church. Or maybe not. Maybe you've had to overcome serious hardships to finally arrive at a place of stability. Maybe Christianity is new to you, but there still aren't many facets of your life others would consider messy or broken. You've likely experienced a mix of joy and sorrow, success and setbacks—though as a whole, life is good. And yet, like me, you're left longing.

This is one of the challenges of so-called good lives—people like us don't always realize the depth of our need. And then when pangs of hunger inevitably grab our attention, we are unsure of how to ease them. When we're not used to suffering, we must learn to seek God through lament. When we're confronted with the seriousness of our not-so-scandalous sins, we must learn to repent and rest in God's grace. When we're faced with the reality of our weakness, we must learn to depend on God. Here is the good news: though hunger pangs may be uncomfortable and even painful at times, they remind us to eat.

As a "good Christian woman" who finds herself increasingly hungry, I want to bring you alongside as we feast at the table God has set for us. There, we will find a God so vast that the universe cannot contain his glory (chapter 1), yet so intimate that he loves us as a father, savior, and friend (chapter 2). His grace is enough to cover all of our failures (chapter 3), and his word protects us from error so that we can truly know him (chapter 4). He is a God who not only enables us to repent of sin (chapter 5), but also sustains us in our weakness (chapter 6). As we walk through life in a fallen world, he offers both abundant joy (chapter 7) and enduring comfort (chapter 8). And because he is a communal God, he blesses us with the fellowship of the church (chapter 9) and sends us on a mission to build his kingdom (chapter 10). He is more than enough to fill our greatest needs and satisfy our deepest longings.

As you read the following pages, my prayer for you echoes Paul's prayer for the Ephesians, "that Christ may dwell in your hearts through faith—that you, being rooted and grounded in love, may have strength to comprehend with all the saints what is the breadth and length and height and depth, and to know the love of Christ that surpasses knowledge, *that you may be filled with all the fullness of God*" (Eph. 3:17–19).

1

Craving Wonder

WE BOARDED THE CABLE CAR alongside a man and his goat. Most nights, the windows would have exposed a mountainous silhouette against a starry sky. Instead, a thick fog lent to the ominous atmosphere of a horror movie as we clanked our way up a cliff toward Gimmelwald, Switzerland—population 130. Unable to see more than a couple of steps ahead of us, we tentatively dragged our suitcases along a dimly lit path until we reached a nearby hostel. Exhausted from a long day of travel (and relieved that we hadn't fallen to our death), we fell right to sleep.

When the sun poured into our room the next morning, we awoke to a stunning view. No longer veiled under the cover of hazy darkness, we were astonished to see the Jungfrau—the highest peak in Europe—perfectly framed within our window. Eager to explore, we rushed through breakfast and questioned our host about the most scenic trails to hike. After laughing at our novice choice of footwear—sneakers instead of hiking boots—he sent us on our way.

The panoramic view was breathtaking from the start. But as the morning mist cleared, allowing us to see further and further into the Alpine mountains, it grew even more stunning. We trekked through twisted and tree-covered trails and came upon clearings that made us halt in wonder. Each time we imagined we'd seen the pinnacle of beauty, we were proven wrong. A new peak would come into view, making the mountain line even more wondrous than before. The vibrantly green grass, blue sky, and snowcapped mountains contrasted so sharply that it almost looked like an overly photoshopped picture. When the afternoon sun danced off the snow, it glimmered like diamonds. Everywhere we turned, we beheld a majestic display of our incomprehensibly wondrous God.

This experience, in many ways, mirrors the wonders of knowing God himself. He is eternally glorious, but apart from the Holy Spirit's work, our hearts are too darkened by sin to see and stand in wonder. Our frail human eyes are blinded to his majesty. Just as my husband and I couldn't grasp the beauty of the Swiss Alps until the sun rose, we cannot grasp the beauty of our Creator until the Holy Spirit illuminates it to us.

And then, in a moment, we *see*. His glory makes us gaze in awe as we walk, for the first time, as children of light. The fog lifts from the morning sky, revealing more of his glory. Though we inevitably traverse dark paths that leave us scraped and scared and worn out, perseverance leads to places where we behold him anew. Just when we think we've got our minds wrapped around him, he shows us more—some peak of beauty we didn't see at first. In him, there is always more to discover.

Our deep soul hunger exists for a reason: we were made to live in wonder.

In this chapter, we will consider how our craving for wonder is meant to draw us to God yet tempts us to seek satisfaction elsewhere. We will also examine three ways to kindle our awe and awaken our worship: enjoying God's creation, remembering God's works, and studying God's attributes.

Distracted from Wonder

God has created us to be filled with wonder, but our lives are often filled with distraction instead. Every year we consume hundreds—if not thousands—of hours of entertainment, binging on cheap amusements instead of curating our selections with a discerning eye for what is lovely and commendable. We mindlessly scroll through social media, lured by clickbait and hot takes, instead of sitting and savoring the sort of good books that help us actually slow down and *think*. We fill our closets and houses with the clutter of insatiable consumerism. Our overcrowded calendars distract us from the rhythms and priorities God designed to cast our eyes upon him and reorient us to his kingdom—too busy with work, sports, and socials, we neglect the Sabbath, fellowship, and serving others.

It's no wonder our hearts grow listless. A. W. Tozer says it well: "Secularism, materialism, and the intrusive presence of things have put out the light in our souls and turned us into a generation of zombies. We cover our deep ignorance with words, but we are ashamed to wonder, we are afraid to whisper 'mystery.'"[1]

We cannot walk as zombies and call it life. When we live in ways that dull our faith, the resulting spiritual boredom enhances the appeal of sin. Created to be filled, we hate feeling empty. It's often in an effort to satiate our longings—or at least to numb them—that we succumb to temptation. We shop in excess to hush our discontented hearts. We entertain lust in our pursuit of pleasure. We chase after accomplishment and recognition in our search for glory. We obsess over our appearance in our quest for beauty. While these pursuits may thrill us at first, they prove futile in the end. Countless wealthy, successful, attractive, respected, famous, intelligent, and hedonistic people can testify to this. We were made to know the living God, and nothing less will satisfy us. When we orient our hearts to behold *him*, he enlivens our dull hearts with wonder. *He* is the source of contentment and pleasure. *He* is the sum of all beauty and glory. When we behold our eternally worthy God, our wonder will never be exhausted.

If my husband and I had just stayed inside and looked through the window, content with only a glimpse of the Swiss Alps instead of going out to explore them, our awe would have waned. Their magnificence wasn't meant to be observed through a 2 x 3–foot piece of glass. In the same way, if we find ourselves uninterested in God, it is because we have stopped exploring. We have limited our view and contented our souls in stuffy rooms rather than stepping out in faith to behold more.

God *delights* to reveal himself to us! He displays his glory in a multitude of ways and invites us to worship with David, "Great is the LORD, and greatly to be praised, and his greatness is unsearchable" (Ps. 145:3).

The Wonder of Creation

God has manifested his glory to the entire world through his creation (Rom. 1:20). As David sang, "The heavens declare the glory of God, and the sky above proclaims his handiwork" (Ps.

19:1). By holding the galaxies in place, he gives us a glimpse of his immense power. Through stars that adorn the night sky and sunsets that paint the horizon, he reveals himself to us. Standing at the summit of a mountain or at the edge of the ocean kindles an awareness of how very small we are. This awareness isn't meant to overcome us with a sense of insignificance, but to fill us with awe of God's magnificence. Our hearts will warm in amazement when we remember that the God who determines the rise and fall of every ocean wave is the God who determines every moment of our days.

As a teenager on a family vacation, I sat outside to spend time in prayer and asked God to show me a shooting star. I wasn't testing him or looking for a sign of his existence; I'd just never seen one and knew he could show me if he wanted to. Over the next half hour he decorated the sky with three! I remember my heart being so moved in wonder—the God in charge of the universe hears *me*! The God who calls every star by name, knows your name too.

It's not just mountain vistas, expansive oceans, and sprawling deserts that display God's majesty. As the artist behind every season, he shows his beauty in flowers and foliage, blue skies and snow-covered fields. He stamps his glory into stones and sand, creeks and waterfalls. He manifests his splendor through iridescent sea creatures, lions roaring across the savanna, blithe mountain goats scaling cliffs, monkeys swinging through rainforests, and eagles soaring the sky. All creatures—great and small, fierce and gentle, cute and creepy—attest to his unmatchable creativity. There are approximately 1.2 million known animal species in the world (scientists estimate the actual number is 8.7 million), and God, *our God*, sustains the life of each one.[2] Every year, new species are discovered. Some boast such striking colors that they stir our imagination about the indescribable beauty awaiting us in the new heavens and the new earth. Others, like the ridiculous-looking blobfish, make us realize that God loves a good laugh.

Most astounding of all, the God who spoke creation into existence also made *us* and bestowed us with the unparalleled honor of bearing his image (Gen. 1:27). Nothing else in the universe—not even the angels—shares this privilege. Our blemishes, wrinkles, quirks, and failures incline us to think otherwise, but *people* are the pinnacle of God's creation. His magnum opus. As he formed Adam from the dust and knit David in the womb, God meticulously crafts each of our bodies and minds and hearts and souls. We are not clones. Because God is worthy of infinite worship, he intentionally designed our differences so that each of our lives can sing to him in a different key. He has given us the capacity to embody his love, justice, truth, and grace, and sovereignly placed us in specific circumstances to do so. And whether we are teachers or lawyers or mothers or writers or doctors or homemakers or students, he has entrusted *us* with the mandate to exercise dominion over the earth (Gen. 1:28–30).

As God's image bearers, we have also been endowed with creativity. So even man-made marvels ultimately point back to him. Consider the engineering required to build the Pantheon without modern construction equipment, or the genius required to send man to the moon—it's nothing short of astonishing. Add to that a seemingly endless array of creative expression in the world. There is a reason that ornate cathedrals, towering skyscrapers, concert halls, and art museums attract scores of visitors—we are drawn to beauty, intrigued by human ingenuity. Created by an infinitely creative God, even food bears the mark of our image bearing. Meals that could be bland and uniform are instead prepared in a mouthwatering symphony of flavors and spices and combinations. Such culinary prowess isn't only achieved in Michelin-star restaurants; one of the best meals I've ever had was cooked in the humble kitchen of a Syrian refugee.

God isn't an elitist who shows beauty only to those who can afford an admission ticket. He manifests his glory among every climate, culture, and class, calling all people to come and worship.

We must take the time to explore and marvel at creation. Go on a hike, watch a nature documentary, study botany, eat your favorite meal, explore your city. Seek whatever captures your heart with awe until you echo the praise due your Creator: "Worthy are you, our Lord and God, to receive glory and honor and power, for you created all things, and by your will they existed and were created" (Rev. 4:11).

The Wonder of His Works

God's marvelous works are meant to incite our awe. This is why he continually instructed the Israelites to remember them. We are called to remember them too. Yet familiarity with the Bible, while vital to the Christian life, brings coinciding challenges. God's mighty deeds fail to move us because we've heard the stories so many times before. Our eyes don't widen the way they did when we first learned of Noah's ark, the parting of the Red Sea, or the tumbling walls of Jericho. Even Jesus's miracles seem like old news.

We must ask God to pierce us through his word and help us marvel at his works. These aren't just stories! They are *real* events, orchestrated by a *real* God, to affect the lives of *real* people. We know this, but our fickle hearts and distracted minds prevent us from meaningful reflection. In an age when we are conditioned to expect quick results, we must learn to patiently steep in Scripture. The Spirit will be faithful to enliven it to us.

And, oh, what glories there are to behold! What wondrous works our God has done! So faithful was God to Daniel that he shut the mouths of ravenous lions meant to devour him (Dan. 6:21–22). So merciful was he to David that he sent Nathan to pluck him from the destructive path paved by his lust and violence (2 Sam. 12:1–15). So inclined was his ear to the poor that he avenged the injustice of Sodom (Ezek. 16:49–50). And then this mighty God condescended to become a humble man (Phil. 2:6–7). So powerful that he could walk on water and calm a raging storm with a word (Matt. 8:26; 14:25). So compassionate that he healed a despised leper and cast a demon out of a Gentile woman's daughter (Matt. 8:3; Mark 7:29). So loving that he stretched out his hands to die for his enemies (Rom. 5:8). So victorious that he defeated death itself (1 Cor.15:55). So worthy that John—during his mysterious foretaste of heaven—recounts, "I heard every creature in heaven and on earth and under the earth and in the sea, and all that is in them, saying, 'To him who sits on the throne and to the Lamb be blessing and honor and glory and might forever and ever!'" (Rev. 5:13).

Not only are God's marvelous works woven in Scripture; they are evident throughout the history of the church and in our own lives as well. Yet we often fail to recognize them. Even though we intellectually believe in his sovereign control, we functionally separate his hands from our daily lives. We shouldn't. God is providentially at work in all of our circumstances.

I recently started a master's program in theological studies. A few years ago, I never would have imagined pursuing a graduate degree. Our budget was too tight, my husband's job offered no path for career growth, and I aspired to write books. It was only after a steady stream of rejected book proposals that I began to consider the idea of seminary. If I wanted to serve others through writing, perhaps I needed to grow as a student of Scripture first. Meanwhile, my husband finally left his job to start a business. He barely brought any money home that first year, and our financial pressure increased—we couldn't possibly afford tuition. Sometime later, I finally had a publisher, my husband's business took off, and after much prayer, counsel, and affirmation, I enrolled in classes. Behind the scenes, God was working in every detail. Had I gotten a publisher the first (or second, or third, or fourth) time I tried, I doubt I would have ever considered seminary. If my husband hadn't spent years feeling stuck in an unfulfilling job, he probably wouldn't have taken the leap to start his own business. This was God's plan for us. In perfect wisdom, he ordained every single delay and disappointment for his good purposes. Nothing in our lives is left to chance. We can trust that our suffering, setbacks, and successes are all ordained by God to lead us where he wills and conform us into his image.

And that is just an example! Think about your life. If you begin to follow the threads of your circumstances, you will see story after story of God caring for you, providing for you, and working through you. You'll find that he often works in ways you didn't expect (and probably didn't want). We won't get to see the full picture now. But in heaven, we will learn how our stories were woven through generations and generations. God is intimately involved with every aspect of our lives, and in perfect wisdom, power, and love he is orchestrating a story written before time began. The more we train our eyes to notice God's marvelous works, the more our hearts will sing:

> Oh give thanks to the Lord; call upon his name;
> > make known his deeds among the peoples!
> Sing to him, sing praises to him;
> > tell of all his wondrous works!
> Glory in his holy name;
> > let the hearts of those who seek the Lord rejoice. . . .
> Remember the wondrous works that he has done,
> > his miracles, and the judgments he uttered.
> > > (Ps. 105:1–3, 5)

The Wonder of His Attributes

Low views of God lead to spiritual despondency, so we must cultivate our wonder by studying his attributes. It is not by the sheer force of will that we stand in awe. When our souls are most hungry and despairing, we must fill our minds with truth too wonderful to comprehend, even though it may not affect us immediately. There is darkness in and outside of us which sometimes clouds God's greatness—grief, trial, temptation, disaster—so we must keep seeking him in faith. He will reveal his glory again, opening our eyes to see him anew.

To be clear, I do not mean to indicate that we discover anything *new* about him. Rather, we only discover what already *is*. God is eternal and unchanging; "Jesus Christ is the same yesterday and today and forever" (Heb. 13:8). He cannot grow in character, because his immutable attributes are already perfect. He cannot improve in power or wisdom, because he is the source of all power and wisdom. However, since *our* understanding is not perfect, *we* can grow and improve in our knowledge of him.

Consider those times when old truths hit you in new ways. Perhaps you were suddenly overwhelmed by God's love for you in Christ and the mercy of the cross. Or a verse you'd read dozens of times captured your heart afresh. Or a friend reminded you of some biblical principle or promise, and though you'd heard it before, it clicked for the first time. In those times, God hasn't changed—you have.

Because God is infinite, we can always learn more about him; because we are finite, we will never fully grasp him. God is both knowable *and* beyond our understanding. The more we truly know him, the more we realize how limited our understanding really is. Finite minds cannot comprehend the great I am. We have our confessions and creeds, but even as we hold them, we must admit to mystery. As Scripture says, "Oh, the depth of the riches and wisdom and knowledge of God! How unsearchable are his judgments and how inscrutable his ways! 'For who has known the mind of the Lord, or who has been his counselor?'" (Rom. 11:33–34).

One of my kitchen cabinets stores an array of mismatched containers and lids. When putting leftover food away, this often leads to the frustrating attempt to secure a lid on a container that just won't fit. After fastening the first three corners in place, I can't manage to get the forth one secure without making another corner pop back up. No matter how hard I try, the lid won't close. In some sense, this is how it feels when we try to wrap our minds around difficult doctrines—God simply refuses to fit into a box. Though the Spirit gives us discernment to turn from false teaching and grow in our understanding of him, the "right" doctrines are never as manageable as we'd like. The incarnation—essential to Christian belief—is as certain as it is unfathomable. How could Jesus be both fully God and fully man and not sacrifice any element of either? We *believe* it is true, but we don't *understand* how it works. Our limits are also obvious when we try to understand the Trinity, or the eternity of God, or the sovereignty of God in a world full of evil. We can and should grow in our understanding of each of these doctrines, and yet we will never fully comprehend any of them.

These limits shouldn't make us throw up our hands in frustration. A God who could be fully understood by finite minds would be so small! Our limits should humble us before the Almighty and help us hold fast to the truth that he has revealed about himself in Scripture (for there is no greater pride than dismissing who God says he is and inserting our own opinions of who he should be).

When we accept the tension of knowing and believing without fully understanding, our hearts are moved in wonder. Just think: God's glory is so vast that no man could see him and live, and yet he made a way for us to spend eternity with him. He is so powerful that he spoke the universe into existence, and yet he's so personal that he knows every hair on our heads. He is the sum of all wisdom and righteousness and goodness and truth and justice, the one to whom the angels cry, "Holy, holy, holy" (Isa. 6:3). Theology—the study of God—should never grow stale, for "he is the inexhaustible fountain of all being, all life, all intelligence, all wisdom, all power, all good, and all true happiness in the universe."[3]

Forever and Ever

Even if I were to spend my whole life living in the Swiss Alps, I would never see the entirety of its beauty. And yet these mountains—majestic as they are—are limited. God has determined their peaks and set their boundaries in a specific place, in a country, in a world, in a universe that he holds in the palm of his hand. If something so small can overwhelm us with wonder, how much more can the Maker of heaven and earth when we seek him!

Eternally existing, infinitely worthy, and incomprehensibly great, God's glory is so vast that the whole world cannot contain it. Even eternity won't exhaust our worship. But the more we behold now, the more we can echo with creation the praise due his holy name.

> The heavens declare Thy glory, Lord,
> In every star Thy wisdom shines;
> But when our eyes behold Thy Word,
> We read Thy name in fairer lines.[4]

Discussion Questions

1. Read Colossians 3:1–2. What practical steps can you take to "set your mind on things that are above?" In what ways is your heart lulled by earthly distraction, and how can you minimize those distractions?

2. Read Psalm 145:3–12. What does this passage say about God? How does it call us to respond? Consider verse 5. What can help us meditate on God's glorious splendor and wondrous works?

3. Describe a time that you felt especially aware of God's magnificence. What stirred that awareness?

4. Read Isaiah 46:9–10. How does the truth of God's sovereignty over your life comfort you?

5. Follow the threads of your circumstances—where have you seen God's providential hands at work?

6. Consider the attributes of God such as his omniscience, self-sufficiency, immutability, wisdom, faithfulness, justice, mercy, love, and holiness. Which of his attributes most move your heart to worship? Which of his attributes do you most struggle to comprehend?

Recommended Reading

A. W. Tozer, *The Knowledge of the Holy* (New York: Harper Collins, 1978).

Jen Wilkin, *None Like Him: 10 Ways God Is Different from Us (and Why That's a Good Thing)* (Wheaton, IL: Crossway, 2016).

2

Craving Love

I LOVE A GOOD ROMANCE and have watched BBC's five-hour production of *Pride and Prejudice* at least ten times. Maybe I should be embarrassed by this. I'm not. Every human heart aches for love, so of course we enjoy a good story about it! Countless songs have been sung, books have been written, and movies have been made exploring this theme. Sometimes the love portrayed is nothing more than a shallow rendering, revealing how much sin has contorted the concept. But there are plenty of honest portrayals of love too. Whether centered on romance or family or friendship or community, the best stories depict sacrificial and enduring love. The kind that is faithful and deep. The kind we all crave.

Life Is Beautiful is one of my favorite films. Set in Italy in 1939, it tells the story of Guido, a young Jewish man. Through several humorous and cleverly devised circumstances, Guido secures the heart of a woman named Dora. They marry, have a son, and run a small bookstore in an idyllic town. They should have lived happily ever after. But the plot takes a tragic turn when the entire family is seized and sent to a concentration camp. During their imprisonment, Guido goes to great lengths to convey signals of love to his wife, who resides separately in the women's sector of the camp. The story's main focus, though, is how Guido protects and nurtures his beloved son amid their captivity. While the romance at the beginning of the film was sweet and heartwarming, it is Guido's dedicated love for his family in the concentration camp that proves most powerful.[6]

As image bearers of God, we cannot help but be gripped by this kind of love. Since God *is* love, we carry love's blueprints on our hearts—shallow imitations inevitably leave us empty.

In this chapter, we will look at the dangers and disappointments of misplaced love and the contrasting perfection of God's love, which he lavishly pours out as our Savior, friend, Father, and Helper.

The Problem of Misplaced Love

Our craving for love is good, for we were *made* to be known intimately and loved faithfully. However, when misplaced, this craving becomes deeply destructive. We idolize friendships and are left embittered when our friends inevitably let us down. We chase after fleeting passion and fall to sexual sin. Desiring ease in our relationships, we recoil from the cost of forgiveness, faithfulness, and perseverance when they get hard. We place our worth in human approval and are devastated when we don't receive it. We expect others to fill us in a way that only God can, and then resent them for falling short.

Not only does misplaced love lead us into sin; it shatters us with disappointment. While many of us enjoy the rich blessings of loving relationships among our families, friends, and churches, even the truest love we receive from others will fail to fill us. In small ways and big, people let us down. People break our trust. People sin against us (just as we sin against them). And sometimes our relationships break beyond repair. Love between fallen people always brings pain, and the only way we can bear it is if we seek to be filled with God's love first. Without his love as our source, we are unequipped to love anyone well. Without his love as our ultimate satisfaction, we have a long road of disillusionment ahead.

Only God's love is perfect. Only God's love can satisfy our longing hearts. So we must consider, what is this love actually like? To understand God's love, we can't simply refer to a list of adjectives describing it. We must understand who God *is*.

Loved by a Savior

First, let's consider how God showed his love by becoming our Savior. Jesus enjoyed complete unity and glory within the Trinity. When mankind rebelled, arrogantly declaring mutiny against our Maker, a plan, formed before time began, was set into motion. Jesus, "who, though he was in the form of God, did not count equality with God a thing to be grasped, but emptied himself, taking the form of a servant, being born in the likeness of men. And being found in human form, he humbled himself by becoming obedient to the point of death, even death on a cross" (Phil. 2:6–8).

Love sent Jesus to earth. He saw our hell-bound state and was determined to intervene. While our tongues cursed his name, he was writing a new song to put on them. While our fists shook in anger, his hands were nailed to a cross. While our hearts were dead in sin, his beat so passionately for us that he bore the punishment we deserved. His dying breath breathed life into us.

We can look high and low, and even the most sacrificial expressions of human love cannot compare to the love of our Savior. At the cross, incomprehensible mercy secured our redemption. At the cross, Jesus absorbed the just wrath of God against our sins. Bearing our iniquities, he endured our judgment—justice was served so that we could be saved. At the cross, Jesus bought our forgiveness and lifted our shame. Through the shedding of his blood, we have been washed white as snow. Jesus has removed our dirty rags and covered us with his righteousness so that we can stand before judgment without fear. In him, we are made perfect.

Apart from Jesus, we would have no hope of reconciliation with God, for "there is one mediator between God and men, the man Christ Jesus" (1 Tim. 2:5). Apart from Jesus, we would break under the weight of our guilt and shame. But Jesus came for this very reason, to pour grace upon grace to those who don't deserve it. He was unwilling to let us race to hell unhindered, so he threw his body in front of us and sacrificed himself to save us.

One of the most comforting aspects of being loved by Jesus is that he knows us completely. Even those closest to us don't know everything. They don't see our wicked musings and intentions and desires. *We* can't even see ourselves clearly or understand ourselves fully. But Jesus knows it all. Absolutely nothing is hidden from his sight, *and he loves us anyway*. Pause for a moment and take that in. This isn't a case of Jesus loving us *and then* finding out about all our baggage—when he bore our sins on the cross, he knew exactly how putrid they were. He also knew how damaged our affections for him would be—that even after receiving his gift of salvation, our love would be fickle. And yet our darkest thoughts, deepest sins, and deficient love didn't drive him away. What amazing love!

When we wonder how God feels about us, we must look to the cross, for hanging there is a stunning manifestation of his love (Rom. 5:8). There was no obligation, no ulterior motive, no merely altruistic purpose at work. Jesus sacrificed himself on our behalf because he loved us. He didn't love us because we were lovely but because we were *his*—chosen and beloved even before our first breath. "In this is love, not that we have loved God but that he loved us and sent his Son to be the propitiation for our sins" (1 John 4:10).

Loved by a Friend

God also demonstrates his love as our friend. Honestly, I don't dwell on friendship with God very often. The term seems almost irreverent. And yet it was Jesus who said, "Greater love has no one than this, that someone lay down his life for his friends. You are my friends if you do what I command you. No longer do I call you servants, for the servant does not know what his master is doing; but I have called you friends" (John 15:13–15).

It is an astounding comfort to be called a friend of God. When we think of God as our Savior, or Father, or King, or Lord, there's a vertical emphasis to the relationship—we are the debtors, children, and subjects who are called to submission. In friendship, however, there is a *horizontal* emphasis.

Jesus doesn't only reign and rule over us; he chooses to walk *alongside* us as a "friend of sinners" (see Matt. 11:19). He sympathizes with our weaknesses because he experienced them. He understands the temptations we face because he faced them too. In the same way we talk to our most trusted friend about our struggles, we can talk to Jesus. We can pour out our hearts before him and trust him to handle them gently. And as the only sinless friend we will ever have, he helps us in ways our friends never could.

It would have been easy for Jesus to simply lead from afar. He preached with an authority that garnered the attention of admirers and adversaries alike. His fame spread like wildfire wherever he went. But rather than contenting himself with crowds, he built relationships. He shared meals with men and women who weren't just his followers but his friends. While Scripture doesn't expound on what these friendships looked like, we can prod our imaginations and wonder. Did Jesus make Peter laugh so hard he couldn't breathe? Did Martha teach Jesus the best way to season fish? Did Mary emote to him about the struggles of being a woman in a culture that so often disparaged them? Did Jesus and his disciples love a good competition, and is that why John felt compelled to document how he outran Peter to the tomb (John 20:4)?

We may not know the particulars of Jesus's friendships, but we do know the marks of a loving friend. Friends are dependable and trustworthy. They make us laugh until our sides hurt, and pray for us when our hearts hurt. They celebrate with us and mourn with us. They are attentive listeners who also aren't afraid to admonish us when we need it. They know our likes and dislikes and are familiar with our struggles, dreams, and fears. They bear with our personality quirks (even if they tease us about them), and forgive us when we sin against them. They don't offer empty flattery but timely and truthful encouragement.

That's who Jesus is to us. And unlike our imperfect friends, he never fails.

Loved by a Father

In perhaps his most tender expression of love, God also loves us as a father. The good news doesn't end with our sins being forgiven. Astounding as the truth is, it gets even better: "When the fullness of time had come, God sent forth his Son, born of woman, born under the law, to redeem those who were under the law, *so that* we might receive adoption as sons" (Gal. 4:4–5). The climax of the gospel isn't forgiveness; it's adoption!

Sin made us orphans. We were utterly helpless and hopeless until the Father came to our rescue. In this, earthly adoption is a powerful picture of the gospel. And yet it is only that—a picture—bearing true but limited similarities to the adoption we have in Christ.

My adopted daughter is no less my child than my two biological sons. She isn't "almost" a part of our family; she *is* family. Likewise we are not "almost" God's children, people saved out of pity who remain on the fringes. We are deeply loved by God, faithfully held in his affections, and forever members of his family.

A key difference between earthly adoption and gospel adoption is that we adopt children who, though sinners, are not responsible for the loss they've endured as orphans. They are suffering the effects of life in a fallen world. We, on the other hand, were enemies of God *because of our sin*. We weren't innocent or abandoned children; we were guilty rebels who abandoned God. Our rebellion—whether manifested through blatant disobedience or godless apathy—nailed God's only begotten Son to a tree. And still, he initiated our adoption.

Now, free from the slavery of sin, God invites us to call him "Father"! He's made us sons and daughters, coheirs with Christ. "And because you are sons, God has sent the Spirit of his Son into our hearts, crying, 'Abba! Father!' So you are no longer a slave, but a son, and if a son, then an heir through God" (Gal. 4:6–7).

My dad is one of my favorite people in the world. Our relationship has been instrumental in forming how I think of God as a father. I associate the title of *father* with respect, trust, closeness, and affection. Yet for many, the concept of God as father is disconcerting. Maybe your father was cold and never showed the affection you craved. Maybe you lived under the perpetual feeling that you were a disappointment to him, no matter how hard you tried to make him proud. Maybe your father's absence or abuse left gaping wounds in your heart. If your earthly father has brought you nothing but heartache, the thought of God as father might make your skin crawl. This is the sting of living in a broken world—it was never supposed to be this way.

When God calls himself our Father, this is what he means: when we are caught in sin, he will rescue us; when we wander as prodigals, he will welcome us home; when we are fearful, he will shelter us; when we are vulnerable, he will protect us; when we are sad, he will wipe our tears; when we are lonely, he will remain near. He shares in all our joys and all our sorrows. He watches over us day and night and pays attention to every detail of our lives. His heart bursts with such love that he rejoices and sings over us (Zeph. 3:17).

God's love for us isn't temperamental or tied to our behavior—it is devoted, passionate, trustworthy, and unchanging. A. W. Tozer expresses God's love in a breathtaking way:

Because God is self-existent, His love had no beginning; because He is eternal, His love can have no end; because He is infinite, it has no limit; because He is holy, it is the quintessence of all spotless purity; because He is immense, His love is an incomprehensibly vast, bottomless, shoreless sea before which we kneel in joyful silence and from which the loftiest eloquence retreats confused and abashed.[7]

The Father will never forsake us. Once you have been brought into his family, he won't let you go.

Loved by a Helper

Finally, let's look at how God expresses his love as our Helper. It's been said that the Holy Spirit—the third person of the Trinity—is sometimes treated as the strange uncle of the family. We're not really sure how to interact with him, so we hope he stays in the corner of the room at holiday gatherings. God the Father and God the Son are easier to embrace because we have earthly representations of those titles. The Holy Spirit? The name almost carries an air of superstition. We might heartily acknowledge his *work*, yet feel uneasy when we meditate on him as a *person* of the Godhead—*someone* who loves us. However, in order to grasp the depths of God's love for us, it's vital to understand the love expressed through the Holy Spirit.

Eternally existing, the Holy Spirit manifested in a unique way after Christ's ascension by coming to dwell *within* all of God's people (Rom. 8:9). He opens our hearts to the gospel and enables us to receive the gift of salvation. He convicts us of sin and helps us turn from temptation as we transform from one degree of glory to another (2 Cor. 3:16–18). And because we fail so often, he comforts us when our consciences condemn us and reminds us of the grace we have in Christ (1 John 3:20). When we struggle with doubt, he gives assurance of salvation and bears witness to our spirit that we are children of God and coheirs with Christ (Rom. 8:16–17; 1 John 3:24). When we don't know how to pray, he intercedes for us (Rom. 8:26). He fills us with the fruit of the Spirit and bestows on us spiritual gifts, strengthening each one of us to nourish the church (1 Cor. 12:4–7; Gal. 5:22–23). He gives us the gift of illumination when we read Scripture, teaching and renewing our minds (John 14:26). All the joys of knowing the Father and the Son are possible only because the Holy Spirit makes God known to us (Eph. 3:14–21).

It was in love that the Spirit came as our Helper. Rather than leaving us alone in this broken world, he chose to dwell *in* us. Always present. Always working. Always helping. Always ministering in times of need. As we eagerly await our resurrected life—when we finally see in full what we now see in part—we can be assured that the Spirit of Christ is with us. We don't have to wait; we can know God intimately now.

Love That Lasts

God's love is so amazing that it seems too good to be true. It tempts us to wonder. Is there a catch? Something we might do to mess things up? The answer is both simple and astounding: *no*.

Our standing before God doesn't rest on the purity of our love but on the perfection of his! Though our love may falter, his always remains faithful. It doesn't ebb and flow based on our obedience. It doesn't play favorites or ever grow cold. Paul reassures us, "I am sure that neither death nor life, nor angels nor rulers, nor things present nor things to come, nor powers, nor height nor depth, nor anything else in all creation, will be able to separate us from the love of God in Christ Jesus our Lord" (Rom. 8:38–39).

God's love for us is steadfast—persistent, unflinching, sure. His heart toward us is gentle, always brimming with compassion and always working for our good. His affections for us are deeper and wider than we can fathom, even higher than the heavens are above the earth. From everlasting to everlasting, in every moment of every day, God's love never ceases—great is his faithfulness.

> Blessed be the God and Father of our Lord Jesus Christ, who has blessed us in Christ with every spiritual blessing in the heavenly places, even as he chose us in him before the foundation of the world, that we should be holy and blameless before him. In love he predestined us for adoption to himself as sons through Jesus Christ, according to the purpose of his will, to the praise of his glorious grace, with which he has blessed us in the Beloved. In him we have redemption through his blood, the forgiveness of our trespasses, according to the riches of his grace. (Eph. 1:3–7)

Discussion Questions

1. In what ways have you experienced the destruction or disappointment of misplaced love? How does being filled with God's love protect you from chasing satisfaction elsewhere?

2. What first comes to mind when you consider God's love? Read Psalm 103:8–13. How does Scripture describe God's love?

3. Read Romans 8:35–39. When are you most tempted to feel as if you've been separated from God's love? What biblical truths are helpful to meditate on in those times?

4. Consider what you learned about how God loves you as Savior, friend, Father, and Helper. Which aspect of his love is most precious to you? Which is hardest for you to believe?

5. Read 1 Corinthians 13:4–7. How does this definition of love compare with worldly ideas of love? In what aspects of love is the Spirit helping you grow? In what ways might he be calling you to repent?

Recommended Reading

Dane Ortlund, *Gentle and Lowly: The Heart of Christ for Sinners and Sufferers* (Wheaton, IL: Crossway, 2020).

Sara Hagerty, *Adore: A Simple Practice for Experiencing God in the Middle Minutes of Your Day* (Grand Rapids, MI: Zondervan, 2020).

3

Craving Grace

IT'S A FAMILIAR STORY. As Jesus reclines at a table with Simon, a notoriously sinful woman abruptly enters the home. Weeping, she falls before him. In a manner that would stir discomfort in any respectable Jewish man, she kisses Jesus's feet, drenches them with tears, wipes them with her hair, and anoints them with expensive oil. Eyes ablaze and mouth agape, Simon is appalled that Jesus would endure such scandalous treatment. Knowing his thoughts, Jesus shares a story: "A certain moneylender had two debtors. One owed five hundred denarii, and the other fifty. When they could not pay, he cancelled the debt of both. Now which of them will love him more?" (Luke 7:41–42). Simon rightly answers: the one who had been forgiven a larger debt. Driving his illustration home Jesus concludes, "Therefore I tell you, her sins, which are many, are forgiven—for she loved much. But he who is forgiven little, loves little" (Luke 7:47).

It is a beautiful story. It should make us marvel at grace. It should incite awe of our Savior. Yet when I used to read it, I'd feel discouraged. I imagined that my "good record" must disqualify me from ever loving Jesus as deeply as others did.

When we have spent many years in the church, been Christians since childhood, or have simply lived scandal-free lives, it's easy to fall into the trap of thinking we are like the debtors who have been forgiven only a little. We hear dramatic testimonies of those saved from lifestyles of addiction or promiscuity or drunkenness or brazen greed and are left feeling almost jealous. They see such a clear contrast between death in sin and life in Christ. They know how to feast at the table of God's grace. We don't, and feel as if we're missing out. However, the problem isn't our good record. The problem is our shallow understanding of our depravity.

In this chapter we will see why grasping the depth of our wickedness is essential to grasping the depth of God's grace. We have been forgiven an egregious debt, and because of that, we can love much. Through the gospel, God gives us the grace we so desperately crave.

The Seriousness of "Respectable Sins"

Our sin is far more serious than we realize. As "good people," we usually battle what the late Jerry Bridges coined as "respectable sins"—sins like discontentment, ingratitude, pride, selfishness, irritability, anger, lack of self-control, impatience, and envy.[8] Though we know we should repent of such tendencies, they don't seem very harmful, so we try to merely tame them instead. We get rid of the temper but feed bitterness. We give our time but hoard our money. We avoid drunkenness but indulge in gluttony. It's not so much outright hypocrisy, because we really *do* want to follow God. The problem is that we focus so much on addressing obvious manifestations of sin that we train its subtle expressions to remain hidden in our hearts. And like any untreated weed or undetected cancer, hidden sins don't die; they grow.

Even in my richest seasons of devotion and love for God, sin has hardened my heart and darkened my mind so abruptly that I know I am *capable* of just about anything—I'm one bad day away from self-inflicted disaster. The destructive beast of sin cannot be tamed, and it's dangerous to treat its "respectable" expressions casually. Jealousy of a coworker can grow so spiteful that we realize we're capable of spreading slanderous lies. Bitterness toward our spouse can grow so vindictive that we realize we're capable of adultery. Seeking refuge in a glass of wine instead of God can become so habitual that we realize we're capable of alcoholism. Unchecked irritation toward our kids can morph into a rage so intense that we realize we're capable of abuse. Even if we have never committed certain sins, knowing we are capable of them should keep us humble. We wholly depend on the grace of God to resist temptation and repent of failure.

Outside of the sins we're capable of, we must also grapple with the gravity of the sins we have committed. If hate is akin to murder, my life is marred by trails of carnage. If lust is akin to adultery, infidelity has stained my marriage. If rash words are like sword thrusts, I have wounded many with my sharp tongue.

My "clean record" is not so clean after all. Neither is yours.

Any time we think that our not-so-messy lives are a barrier to loving Christ deeply, it is because we have forgotten our depravity. Or perhaps we have never even recognized it. On the outside we may look good, but in comparison to a holy God, we are and always will be desperate for grace.

God's righteous anger burns so hotly against sin that the only way to quench it—without compromising holy justice—was to send his Son to drink the cup of wrath in our stead. Jesus didn't just endure death on behalf of murderers, adulterers, and thieves. Our "respectable" sins required the sacrifice of blood too. He died for complainers and glory-seekers and little-white-liars. He stretched out nail-scarred hands because we were tightfisted toward the poor. He wore a crown of thorns because we adorned ourselves with arrogance. The lashes on his back, blood on his brow, and desperation of his cry testified to the great cost of our salvation.

Our sin sent Jesus to the cross just as much as the criminal nailed beside him. "For *all* have sinned and fall short of the glory of God, and are justified by his grace as a gift, through the redemption that is in Christ Jesus, whom God put forward as a propitiation by his blood, to be received by faith" (Rom. 3:23–25).

Late theologian R. C. Sproul has called sin "cosmic treason" against God.[9] This is an important concept to grasp. We don't just make mistakes; we rebel. We don't just act in weakness; we act in wickedness. We know the one worthy of all praise, yet we still fashion idols to worship. We bow before success, money, power, and approval. We worship our desires and dreams so much that we willingly disobey God's decrees to attain them.

In the Old Testament God calls the nation of Israel a whore for its idolatry. A *whore*—one of the most derogatory terms in our language. It seethes with disdain and reeks of guilt. It demonstrates that loving *anything* more than God—even good things like family or ministry or recreation—is the same as committing adultery against God. He is jealous for our affections, and rightly so. He is not some insecure being thirsting after approval; he is incomparably glorious and desires our worship because he loves us, and worship is what we were *created* to do.

To the world we may seem good. To the world our sins might not seem like a big deal. After all, everyone is a little messy. But when we draw near to a holy God, our sin isn't something to laugh off, belittle, or justify because "nobody's perfect." Our sins are so wicked that they deserved God's eternal wrath. Our hearts are so depraved that they couldn't just be fixed; they needed to be made new.

It doesn't matter if you became a Christian at four or forty, if you have been addicted to approval or addicted to porn, if you have sought escape in Netflix or in drunkenness—before God, there is no such thing as a good record. Our debt is deeper than we can imagine, and it cost the Son of God his blood for us to be forgiven.

His Grace Is Greater than We Can Imagine

Understanding the seriousness of our sin is not meant to bludgeon us with guilt. Rather, it's to enable us "to comprehend with all the saints what is the breadth and length and height and depth" of God's love (Eph. 3:18). Only when we recognize the magnitude of sin can we understand just how good the good news is.

Though at one time we were enemies of God, now we are called friends. Though we were children of wrath, now we are children of the Father. Though we were running headfirst to hell, now we await eternal life in heaven. Though we were dead in our sins, we have been made alive by the Spirit. Though we—like Israel—played the whore, now we are the bride of Christ.

What good news! All the sins we have already committed—and all the sins we will commit—have been paid for in full. "There is therefore now no condemnation for those who are in Christ Jesus" (Rom. 8:1). We do not have to bend or break under the weight of our guilt. Jesus has lifted the burden of our shame and covered us with his righteousness. Because we are hidden in Christ, God doesn't look at us and well up with wrath; he looks at us and wells up with love. Think of it—marvel at it. Even when we sin, *God wells up with love.* That doesn't mean our sin has ceased to be grievous. It is just as wicked now as it ever was—perhaps even more so since we have tasted and seen that God is good and still choose to return to filth. But now, instead of a judge ready to drop his gavel and declare our punishment, we have a father who graciously leads us to repentance. He convicts our hearts of sin, he shows us the way of righteousness, he strengthens us to obey. Even the discipline we endure is just another demonstration of grace, "for the Lord disciplines the one he loves, and chastises every son whom he receives" (Heb. 12:6).

God's grace runs so deep that we could never outrun him in our guilt. He is a relentless rescuer who seeks us when we hide, covers us when we fail, and clings to us when we fall. And when we come to him in tears—broken by the way we have betrayed him yet again—he treats us with the same tenderness that he treated the sinful woman. He doesn't look at us churched people and bellow that we should know better by now. He doesn't berate us, or condemn us, or crush us. He draws near to help. The lover of our souls will not abandon us to sin.

> For as high as the heavens are above the earth,
>> so great is his steadfast love toward those who fear him;
> as far as the east is from the west,
>> so far does he remove our transgressions from us.
> As a father shows compassion to his children,
>> so the LORD shows compassion to those who fear him.
>> (Ps. 103:11–13)

Even if we walk as prodigals, he remains the Father who stands at the doorstep, awaiting our return—not to slam the door on us, but to throw us a party. He delights when wandering children return to fellowship with him.

Living as a prodigal does not necessarily entail outward and obvious disobedience. The hearts of "good" Christians can drift just as far as those who imitate the blatant rebellion of the Prodigal Son. Our lives might not spin out of control, but we can grow just as callous and resentful toward our Father. We may remain involved at church while inwardly and incessantly brooding over our circumstances. We may not deny our faith but find we barely care about it anymore. And before long—whether due to apathy or dogged bitterness—our lips cease praying, our Bibles become dusty, and our hearts grow numb.

When we go through these seasons of rebellion, God is not repulsed by our rage. He isn't frustrated with us or even surprised. He isn't scrambling to justify himself against our barrage of arrogant accusations. When we kick and scream against him, he holds us with a firm gentleness. Our love for him may vanish for a while, but his love does not waver. Once grace is lavished upon us, his love will never leave us.

In Christ, it is *impossible* for our sin to separate us from the love of God.

We Can Love Him More than We Thought

As sinners who have been forgiven a debt far greater than we could imagine, our capacity to love Christ can grow deeper each day. We will never worry that we can't love as much as the sinful woman in Luke's Gospel, once we learn to identify with her.

As we mature in faith, pressing closer and closer toward the light of the world, the shadows that keep us from seeing the depth of God's grace will diminish. Our perspective will sharpen, allowing us to marvel at the way he has met our anger with patience, our discontent with satisfaction, our bitterness with mercy, our selfishness with self-sacrifice. Our persistent struggles serve as a backdrop to highlight the love and forgiveness of Christ. Closeness to him exposes us, giving us a vivid picture of his extravagant mercy and our desperate need. And, oh, how could this striking contrast not ignite our love?

Knowing our propensities to wander, it is imperative to stir our love by engaging in the spiritual disciplines that draw us to him. We must remain in the word—meditating on it, studying it, listening to it preached—and pray that our hearts would see God. We must also pursue fellowship with other Christians, because God uses their prayers, encouragement, admonishment, and correction to protect us from drifting away. And when we are in the valley and the gospel fails to touch us, and our hearts feel cold toward the wonders of his grace, we can press forward with hope.

We are not the first people to beg God, "Restore to me the joy of your salvation, and uphold me with a willing spirit" (Ps. 51:12).

There is a day coming when our love for God will be unhindered by sin or weakness, when it will only and ever grow in the light of his presence. But until that day, when we finally take our last breath and wake up to new life in eternity, God will be faithful. The Holy Spirit will empower us to love him more today, to love him more now, to love him more here.

> Your worst days are never so bad that you are beyond the reach of God's grace. And your best days are never so good that you are beyond the need of God's grace.[10]

Discussion Questions

1. Read Luke 7:36–50. When have you most identified with the sinful woman in Luke's Gospel? What hinders you from loving Christ as one who has been forgiven much?

2. What "respectable sins" are most common in your life? Why are you tempted to tolerate them? How can you seek to put them to death?

3. When does your sin tempt you toward condemnation? How can you turn your eyes upon Jesus and rest in his grace?

4. Read Romans 8:1. What other Scripture verses remind you of Jesus's forgiveness?

5. How can you cultivate gratitude for God's grace? How might that help you love him more?

Recommended Reading

Jerry Bridges, *The Discipline of Grace: God's Role and Our Role in the Pursuit of Holiness* (Colorado Springs, CO: NavPress, 1994).

Timothy Keller, *The Prodigal God: Recovering the Heart of the Christian Faith* (New York: Viking, 2008).

4

Craving Truth

IF I DRINK COFFEE after noon, it keeps me awake at night. I've been this way for years. Nevertheless, when I'm craving an extra dose of espresso or can't resist the offer of a latte, I convince myself that I'll sleep just fine. Later, after tossing and turning in bed for hours, I regret my decision. Even though I *knew* what would happen, I convinced myself it wouldn't—I denied my well-established sensitivity to caffeine because I didn't want to deny my palate. Always exhausted the next day, I chide myself for my foolishness. The latte wasn't worth it.

Anytime we disregard truth, there are consequences. As far as my caffeine consumption, the cost is only minor and temporary. But when we're talking about the inerrant truth of God's word, the consequences are far more serious.

From the beginning of time, humankind has had a particular talent for rejecting truth. It started in the garden, continued after the flood, and drove kings to madness and disgrace. The truth rejected changes person to person, culture to culture, century to century, but the rebellion behind it is the same—man wants to take the place of God, to judge what is good and what is evil. God warns through the prophet Isaiah, "Woe to those who call evil good and good evil, who put darkness for light and light for darkness, who put bitter for sweet and sweet for bitter!" (Isa. 5:20).

Between the sin of our own hearts, the seductive deception of the world, and the sinister enemy of our souls, we must be on guard. Scripture tells us to "be sober-minded; be watchful. Your adversary the devil prowls around like a roaring lion, seeking someone to devour" (1 Pet. 5:8). If we presume that our church background or theological convictions are enough to guard us from drift or apostasy, we are in danger. The Israelites were witnesses to miracles and deliverance—they *knew* the living God—and still they fell away. Repeatedly. After referencing their wayward example, Paul cautions, "Therefore let anyone who thinks that he stands take heed lest he fall" (1 Cor. 10:12). This doesn't mean that we should walk crippled by fear but that we should walk *aware* of the dangers around and within us. Faith in God's preserving grace should never lead to a presumption that we cannot wander.

We are desperate for truth, precisely because we are desperate for God—for he *is* the truth (John 14:6). We cannot love him unless we know who he really is, and we cannot follow him unless we know what he has called us to do. It's impossible to understand true justice, holiness, purity, or love apart from him, because he is their very source.

In this chapter, we will examine various deceptions we are prone to consume and our crucial need to be filled with God's word. As we stand on the sure footing of Scripture and set our gaze upon

Jesus, he will expose the lies that seduce us and lead us on the path of righteousness.

Our Hearts Are Deceitful

We have been born as sinful beings in a sinful world. Prior to salvation, we are ruled by darkness—after salvation, we are still lured by it. As Paul writes, "The desires of the flesh are against the Spirit, and the desires of the Spirit are against the flesh, for these are opposed to each other, to keep you from doing the things you want to do" (Gal. 5:17).

In Christ, we *can* discern good from evil, obedience from rebellion, righteousness from unrighteousness. Because the Holy Spirit dwells within us and God's word instructs us, our minds and hearts can be transformed by truth. As we walk in humility before God, he will set a steady path for our feet.

The problem is, we are tempted to trust ourselves more than God. And when we do, disaster ensues. Like the Israelites, we begin to do what is right in our own eyes (Judg. 21:25). As persistent self-justifiers, we cannot trust ourselves with this much power. Only God has the wisdom and authority to determine what is right. While the world tells us to follow our hearts and define our own truth, we must heed Jeremiah's warning: "The heart is deceitful above all things, and desperately sick; who can understand it?" (Jer. 17:9). Sin-sick hearts can't be trusted, but they can be *treated* with the healing balm of God's word.

However, even when we intellectually believe in the inerrancy of God's word and its authority over our lives, our heart sickness still manifests in subtle ways. We make subtle excuses for sin: *If you knew how terrible my day was, you'd understand why I got a little drunk that night.* We embrace subtle lies: *I don't need to confess to anyone how I've been struggling with this sin—I can get it under control by myself.* And we subtly reject truth: *I don't need the church. I love Jesus, and that's all that matters.* Nobody throws theological convictions aside rashly; drift takes time. While this drift might happen under the influence of others, it often springs from our own desires. We deny and disobey because we *want*. We are endlessly creative at finding justifications for sin.

This is especially true with persistent struggles. I don't succumb to jealousy often, so when I do, it grabs my attention. I see it for its ugliness and seek God's help, and he empowers me to repent. But anger—this sin has plagued me since childhood. Rarely one to start an argument but always one to end it, I have mastered the art of the blame-shift (after all, *they* started it). I get along with most people but can ruthlessly nurse bitterness once I've been wronged. Motherhood adds its own daily trickle of temptation, because, low and behold, my children are sinners just like me. And too often, when my idolatrous desire for a peaceful home collides with another sibling rivalry, I react with anger. Such persistent failure is discouraging, so to assuage my conscience I often try to justify my sin. It's easier than confessing *again*.

But, oh, what havoc is wreaked on our lives when we stop confessing and start entertaining our deceitful hearts! Under the cover of pride, sin thrives.

If we don't see the deceitfulness of our own hearts, we won't have the humility to fight it. Puffed up in our own wisdom, we will neglect the help God provides to fortify our faith. We will stifle the voice of the Holy Spirit and silence the conviction of

Scripture. And when faithful friends speak into our lives with piercing precision, we will resent them. Sin hates the light. If we let it fester in our hearts, we will increasingly love the dark and resist anything that tries to expose us. Humble confession, fellowship with other Christians, and accountability to a local church are vital safeguards to keep us from wandering.

The Lure of Compromise

We live in an increasingly secularized society, and we shouldn't panic when unbelievers reject truth. Why would strangers of Jesus trust what he says? However, for the integrity, holiness, and witness of the church, we *should* be concerned that so many professing Christians unabashedly tamper with Scripture. Some erase hell. Some celebrate greed and sexual sin. Some affirm multiple paths to God and deny Christ's substitutionary atonement. Rejecting the freedom that's found in submission to Christ, they seek freedom in self-actualization, self-achievement, and self-expression—self is the new golden calf.

Though some of these damned doctrines might not entice us, others could. No one is impervious to deception. Paul's sobering words still ring true today: "The time is coming when people will not endure sound teaching, but having itching ears they will accumulate for themselves teachers to suit their own passions" (2 Tim. 4:3). We are all prone to itching ears, and there is a range of false teaching appealing to them. We must immerse ourselves in Scripture and humbly seek the Spirit's help to discern doctrinal truth from error.

This isn't just about knowing the right answers, it's about loving the true God. God has commanded that we love him with all of our heart, soul, mind, and strength—in other words, our *entire* beings. And it seems that most of our drift into false teaching happens when we compromise in one of those areas. As we consider three common temptations, ask God to reveal where you are most vulnerable to compromise.

Compromising the Mind: The Thinkers

One way we are tempted to compromise truth is by relying on our own intellect. If we are uncomfortable with certain aspects of God's word, we try to adapt it. Every modern heresy is just an old lie that's been repackaged—there is nothing new under the sun (Eccles. 1:9). Appealing to different appetites, they derive from the same seed. As Satan seduced Eve in the garden, they all whisper, "Did God *really* say?"

It is this question that has led to an endless string of deconversion stories—people who used to confess orthodoxy deconstruct their faith, denying or twisting any portion of Scripture that cannot coexist with their newfound belief system. This is not just a difference in doctrinal convictions, for there is plenty of room for God-fearing, Bible-believing Christians to learn and grow and disagree. We *should* have robust and charitable debate over important issues like baptism, the continuation of spiritual gifts, women's roles in the church, missiology, and predestination. We should be able to hold firm convictions while having respect for those who sit on the other side of a particular issue—and we should be willing to change our views anytime we're convinced that there is a more faithful way to align them with Scripture. In all of this, we must humbly embrace mystery, for the word itself claims that God is unsearchable.

Maturing in faith always deepens humility, because the more we know God, the more we realize how much there is to learn. Yet that is precisely what makes this sort of compromise difficult to identify as dangerous—questions and fluid belief systems *appear* humble. Furthermore, the prince of darkness hails himself as an angel of light—the lies he whispers *seem* good (2 Cor. 11:14). But the moment we undermine the inspiration, inerrancy, and authority of Scripture and enshrine our own opinions, we have ceased to be truth seekers and sought to become truth definers. *That* is the height of pride.

Our humility should always be postured toward God before it is postured toward people. It is *not* humility to deny biblical teachings when we don't like them or fear offending others. It is *not* humility to be ambiguous where Scripture is clear. It is *not* humility to just "agree to disagree" about essential doctrines of the faith. True humility is believing God and submitting to his truth and authority.

But we tend to equate strong convictions with being close-minded, especially when others claim we're just victims of the "Christian machine." Nobody wants to be a cog in a machine, so when we hear these accusations, we begin to second-guess ourselves: *Maybe I haven't asked enough questions. Maybe I am being led by my church tradition instead of eternal truth. Maybe I do need to rethink this.*

And it's true—*maybe we do.* We should passionately devote ourselves to the study of the word and wrestle with God through our doubts. But wrestling and questioning and digging must be rooted in a submissive desire to discover what God *actually* says, not what we want him to say. A. W. Tozer puts it well:

[The Christian scholar] may compare Scripture with Scripture until he has discovered the true meaning of the text. But right there his authority ends. He must never sit in judgment upon what is written. He dare not bring the meaning of the Word before the bar of his reason. He dare not commend or condemn the Word as reasonable or unreasonable, scientific or unscientific. After the meaning is discovered, the meaning judges him; never does he judge it.[11]

Deep and difficult questions, when asked with hearts submitted to God's authority, won't lead to the unraveling of our faith. Rather, they are the bulwark that will root us and guard us from heresy. Good questions help good theology go deeper.

So rather than stifling your questions, wrestle through them. God gives us a hunger for truth, and he fills us through his written word. Scripture might not reveal everything we wish to know, but it does reveal everything we *need* to know. As we study it with humility, asking the Spirit to renew our minds, it will prove a steady anchor that keeps us from being "tossed to and fro by the waves and carried about by every wind of doctrine" (Eph. 4:14).

Compromising the Heart: The Feelers

Many of us are tempted to compromise truth because of our own feelings. This temptation tends to lure those who have a genuine care for others and roots its falsity under the guise of compassion. True and biblical principles, such as the priorities of caring for the poor, defending the vulnerable, and seeking justice for the oppressed, are emphasized *at the expense* of other and equally important biblical truths.

Those in this camp talk about love and grace a lot but rarely about our need for repentance or the reality of God's wrath. They talk about building longer tables and breaking down barriers, championing an indiscriminate faith that requires no repentance or redeemer. They dismiss that Jesus preached a narrow way to escape the flames of hell and that our welcome hinges on his rescue.

I can identify with these temptations. Since childhood I have been passionate about showing mercy to the needy, a conviction that God only deepens. Though I'm grateful for his work, it has forced me to wrestle through certain doctrines in painful ways. As I've built close relationships with Muslim refugees—people who have already endured unconscionable suffering—it is emotionally agonizing to remember that they remain under God's wrath. If they do not repent of their sins and turn to Christ for salvation, they will suffer eternal damnation. Instinctively, I don't want to believe it. But Jesus was clear: "I am the way, and the truth, and the life. No one comes to the Father except through me" (John 14:6). Allah cannot save them. A welcoming community cannot save them. A seat at the table cannot save them. Only Jesus can. So if I truly love them, I must show it in action and in truth. I must preach the *real* gospel, the *whole* gospel, the *true* gospel; a partial gospel is no gospel at all.

We are rarely drawn away by blaring errors. Usually, we drift into what *feels* right because portions of it *are* right. Even Satan tempted Jesus using Scripture. If we aren't watchful, we will fail to discern when doctrine is bent just enough to become deadly and when beautiful language masks grotesque lies. Often these contortions spring from believing a man-centered gospel rather than a God-centered one. People, their feelings, and their perceptions of good are placed over God, his commands, and what is actually good. When the gospel is a proclamation of *our* worthiness, *our* value, *our* belonging, we have missed the whole point. The good news of the gospel is that *despite* our unworthiness, *God* is so good, so loving, so merciful that he made a way to save us through *Jesus*.

When the gospel is centered on man instead of God, affirming sinful desires is the inevitable by-product. In recent years, this has largely played out in the affirmation of unbiblical sexual ethics. On the one hand, I think it's true that the church needed correction for its treatment of people who identify as LGBTQ+. We may have walked in truth, but we often lacked grace. We had brothers and sisters struggling alone, scared to even give voice to their temptations, and we must consider *why*. We alienated lost sinners because of their sin rather than telling them of the God who died to save them. We are called to be gentle and compassionate toward anyone trapped in sin, as Christ has been to us. Truth may be offensive to those whose hearts aren't softened by the Spirit, but may it never be said that our unloving behavior was a barrier to the gospel. We must value the dignity of all God's image bearers—including those who sin or are tempted in different ways from us—and treat them with love. We cannot preach the hope of a Savior—the hope sinners *need* for true repentance—if we are too busy being self-righteous.

We must also remember that the greatest problem of unbelievers who reject God's design for sex and gender is not the particular sins they practice. It's that they are separated from God. Their greatest need is not to be made straight, but to be made sons and daughters of the Father. As Jackie Hill Perry writes:

For the unbeliever that is [same-sex attracted], God is not mainly calling them to be straight; He's calling them to Himself. To know Christ, love Christ, serve Christ, honor Christ, and exalt Christ, forever. When He is the aim of their repentance, and the object of their faith, they are made right with God the Father and given the power by the Holy Spirit to deny all sin—sexual and otherwise.[12]

Oh, compassionate Christian, don't be fooled into thinking that love for our neighbor means we must divorce from truth! Without the guardrails of truth to guide us, we will *fail* at loving others. Love is defined by God, not by our opinions. Becoming an advocate and ally of sin is *never* the answer. Any claim that someone can live in unrepentant sin—sexual or otherwise—and love Jesus is not just misguided; it is a rebellious denial of Jesus's declaration, "If you love me, you will keep my commandments" (John 14:15).

If we truly love our neighbors, we will want them to walk in repentance and follow Jesus as partakers in the kingdom of God. If we truly love our neighbors, we will heed Paul's warning: "You may be sure of this, that everyone who is sexually immoral or impure, or who is covetous (that is, an idolater), has no inheritance in the kingdom of Christ and God. Let no one deceive you with empty words, for because of these things the wrath of God comes upon the sons of disobedience" (Eph. 5:5–6).

Anyone who affirms disobedience to God's word is echoing the slick tongue of the serpent. In the name of love, they encourage us to cling to the sin Christ died to free us from. The gospel of grace breaks the shackles of sin, and real love doesn't encourage us to return to them. "For freedom Christ has set us free; stand firm therefore, and do not submit again to a yoke of slavery" (Gal. 5:1).

Compromising Strength: The Doers

Finally, some of us compromise truth because we're so ambitious for our own goals and desires that we fail to submit to God's word. Wealth, power, prestige, influence, fame—we all want something. Though some of our desires aren't inherently sinful, they become so when they stroke our egos, feed our pride, and stir our craving to gain earthly comfort instead of a cross.

Words spoken in pompous pulpits and best-selling books tell us to claim the futures we want ("in faith," of course). After all, as sons and daughters of the King, we should be recipients of abundance. Meanwhile, it's forgotten that our King wore a crown of thorns and that

> he had no form or majesty that we should look at him,
>   and no beauty that we should desire him.
> He was despised and rejected by men,
>   a man of sorrows and acquainted with grief;
> and as one from whom men hide their faces
>   he was despised, and we esteemed him not.
>
> Surely he has borne our griefs
>   and carried our sorrows;
> yet we esteemed him stricken,
>   smitten by God, and afflicted. (Isa. 53:2–4)

Teaching that discipleship involves suffering and self-sacrifice doesn't appeal to the proud. Preaching that we gain our lives by losing them doesn't evoke thunderous applause from those ambitious for glory. So instead we are told that victorious faith gives us prosperity *now*, success *now*, glory *now*. Work hard, pray hard, and be blessed. Supposedly, we are the directors of our destinies and heroes of our stories, and the only thing getting in the way of an abundant life is us.

To be clear, there *is* abundant life for those found in Christ, and Christians should have a deep-rooted faith that God always acts in goodness toward his children. But he doesn't define abundance in the way the world does. Sometimes healing doesn't come until heaven, sometimes provision looks nothing like we asked, and sometimes blessing comes in the form of suffering. Real abundance is found the closer we get to Jesus, even when it's sorrow that has driven us there.

Many of us see through obvious expressions of name-it-and-claim-it heresy. We may even feel a righteous anger toward the havoc they cause—hurting people who were told their cancer would have been healed if they'd only had more faith or were made to feel as if their poverty was a punishment for not hustling hard enough. But we may not realize how subtly this message has influenced our beliefs. Perhaps we believe that if we parent a particular way, it guarantees our children won't rebel. Or if we walk in purity, we will never endure sexual hurt in marriage. Or if we memorize enough Scripture, we won't struggle with depression. On paper, our doctrine may be sound, but in everyday life, we inadvertently link godly principles of living with promises God never gave. And if we don't recognize our propensity to do this, our faith is susceptible to shattering when trials come our way.

Oh, may our faith grow deep enough to submit to God's sovereignty, may our hard work be done for God's glory, and may our obedience be rooted in love for God!

God's Word Is Truth

Our hearts long for truth. As news sources report conflicting data, experts disagree, conspiracy theories run rampant, friends hold different views, and relativism is the norm, it is stabilizing to know that God's word is truth. It doesn't shift based on popular opinion. It isn't biased or manipulative or twisted by ulterior motives. It doesn't develop over time or depend on outside information. Even the words of the godliest people we know are fallible, but God's word is true about all things, to all people, in all places, at all times. As the psalmist wrote, "The sum of your word is truth, and every one of your righteous rules endures forever" (Ps. 119:160).

It is impossible to gain footing on the subjective sands of "my truth" or "your truth"—the only solid foundation we have is *God's* truth. As many professing Christians undermine the relevance and reliability of Scripture, Paul's words are crucial to remember: "All Scripture is breathed out by God and profitable for teaching, for reproof, for correction, and for training in righteousness, that the man of God may be complete, equipped for every good work" (2 Tim. 3:16–17). Scripture cannot be tampered with or tamed. It is to be studied, believed, and obeyed for God's glory and our good.

Scripture is completely trustworthy. *Everything* it says—its warnings and wisdom, its instruction and correction, its prophecies and promises—is good and trustworthy, because *God* is good and trustworthy.

Scripture is also sufficient. It gives us everything we need for life and godliness. This doesn't mean we can't learn from other sources, but rather that Scripture is the lens from which we must view everything else. It enables us to discern between worldly and godly wisdom, between half-truths and real truth. It is the filter through which we must pour all human observation, opinion, and understanding.

Scripture is so much more than a book about wisdom and righteous living though. It is where God reveals *himself*. If we want to know him better, we are invited to seek him in his word. Don't be discouraged when you don't understand a text. Keep reading! God wants to be known, and when we seek him humbly, he will faithfully increase our understanding. Our finite minds will never know him fully, but we can know him *accurately* through sacred words that impart understanding not just to the scholar, but to the simple (Ps. 119:130).

When we abide in Scripture, the boxes we subconsciously try to squeeze God into break. We find that he is loving, but he is vengeful. He is merciful, but he is just. He saves, but he punishes. He is good, but the earth trembles before him. He is sovereign, but he ordains suffering and allows evil. He reigns in majesty, but he lived as a humble man. And if we are honest, he makes us all a little uneasy. We might be comfortable talking about the extravagance of his goodness and mercy yet feel we need to obscure his anger. Or we are comfortable discussing his righteousness and holiness but worry that emphasizing his extravagant grace leads to irreverent lives that presume upon it. As we abide in Scripture, we must embrace *all* that it says about God—even those things that seem like a paradox.

As Scripture reveals who God is, it also unfolds his plan of redemption. Every page from Genesis to Revelation tells the story of a king who would come to rescue his people and restore his kingdom. This king—Jesus—claimed victory through his death and resurrection, and will bring it to completion when he returns. It's so easy for us to get caught up in our own lives and forget that we are a part of a bigger story. We must read God's word again and again—*cover to cover*—to remind ourselves of who he is, what he has done, and all he has promised to finish. Over time, we will grow to understand how the exhaustive Levitical laws pointed forward to our gracious Savior, and how the genealogies that make our eyes glaze over are actually a beautiful account of God's faithfulness to his covenant. The more familiar we become with the Old and New Testaments and their relationship to each other, the more our hearts will leap as we behold God's redemptive work. This builds our faith when we question God's love, doubt his power, or forget his faithfulness to fulfill his promises. It reminds us that even when it looks like evil has won, the story isn't over. The author of life doesn't make mistakes, and his plan always prevails.

Our Daily Bread

All the dangers that cause drift are mitigated by meditating on God's word. There is truth to minister to every trial, fight every temptation, and impart wisdom to every decision. Scripture is the sustaining sustenance of our souls—our daily bread. Just as runners need to stay hydrated to finish their race, we need the word to finish ours. When we are weary from the trials and temptations of life, it fills up our famished hearts and nourishes them with a truth that is sweeter than honey. And when darkness surrounds us, it will be the lamp to our feet and light to our path (Ps. 119:105) that leads us on the narrow way until Christ brings us home.

> We can't discern what's false if we don't train our eyes on what is true. The best weapon we have for discerning true teaching from false teaching and sin from righteousness is "the sword of the spirit, the Word of God" (Eph. 6:17). The Word of God is a weapon, forged to combat forgery.[13]

Discussion Questions

1. In what ways are you most vulnerable to compromise your heart (the feelers), your mind (the thinkers), or your strength (the doers)? What would it look like to grow in discernment?

2. Read James 1:13–15 and 2 Timothy 4:3–4. What desires tend to entangle us and tempt us to twist or disregard God's word?

3. What are some lies common in our culture today? What biblical truths confront those lies?

4. Read Psalm 119:10–16. How can we cultivate a deeper love for Scripture? How can we help one another in this pursuit?

5. What practical steps have you taken to prioritize studying, memorizing, and meditating on Scripture? In what ways would you like to grow?

Recommended Reading

John Piper, *A Peculiar Glory: How the Christian Scriptures Reveal Their Complete Truthfulness* (Wheaton, IL: Crossway, 2016).

Alisa Childers, *Another Gospel?: A Lifelong Christian Seeks Truth in Response to Progressive Christianity* (Carol Stream, IL: Tyndale, 2020).

5

Craving Change

I SIT DOWN AT MY DESK, open my Bible, and sip my coffee. While I read, I pray for the Holy Spirit to renew my mind and transform my heart to better know, love, and honor him. But as I petition before the throne, my child interrupts for the *fifth* time asking for a snack (even though I gave her breakfast 20 minutes ago). My answer is no, and she leaves with a huff and her hands on her hips. Irritated by the lack of quiet during my "quiet time," I return to prayer and ask God to fill me with grace and patience toward my children. I want to be a mom who reflects the loving forbearance of my Savior. Then I hear my sons yelling at each other. Their voices grow louder as they stomp up the stairs and race into my bedroom, hoping to be the first one to hurl blame on the other. I'd asked for patience only seconds before; now I'm yelling at them, "WILL YOU JUST LEAVE ME ALONE SO I CAN PRAY?"

Similar frustrations reverberate in all sorts of scenarios. Whether we are at home or work or school or church, it seems we can't even pray without the reality of our sin smacking us across the face.

We don't want to be hypocrites.

We really do want to change.

And yet we still sin. We gossip and complain. We feed bitterness and anger. We indulge lust, gluttony, and materialism. We compromise.

Our ongoing sin is discouraging. We wonder how we can love God so much one day and be entirely self-consumed the next. How can we sing with genuine gratitude about his goodness to us and then covet our neighbor's house or accomplishments? How can the same lips that pray, worship, and preach the gospel also wound the people we love most?

It's not only the sin present in our lives that troubles us, but the righteousness that is absent. Our problem isn't always that we do the wrong thing; it's that we *don't* do the right thing. Growth in holiness is not just about killing sin but about cultivating the fruits of righteousness. And when we look at our lives, it's obvious that a good deal of fruit is missing.

This conflict between who we *want to be* and who we *are* is perplexing. The enemy capitalizes on it to condemn us, tempting us with the malicious whispers: *How can you even say you love Christ—you hypocrite! You're a fraud. You'll never change. You'll always sin like this.*

Satan is a liar.

Be encouraged by Paul's words to the church of Philippi: "I am *sure* of this, that he who began a good work in you will bring it to completion at the day of Jesus Christ" (Phil. 1:6). God will not leave you in your sin. He will not forsake the work he started or declare you a lost cause. He is able to keep you from stumbling, and he will present you holy and blameless.

As we'll see in this chapter, anyone in Christ is a new creation. By his grace, we have renewed desires, the freedom to bear fruit, and the strength to fight temptation as we strive toward holiness. We long to change—and because of Christ, we can.

Renewed Desires

To be in Christ is to be a new creation—the old has passed away, the new has come (2 Cor. 5:17). There was a time when we were ruled by sin. We were probably nice neighbors and good friends. We probably made responsible choices and worked hard at our jobs. We may have even been churchgoers or active servants in our community. And yet, enslaved by our own desires, we were totally incapable of loving and submitting to God. When you've built your own kingdom, you don't welcome someone else as king.

But God, being rich in mercy, set us free from the dominion of sin. Though it still ensnares us, it no longer rules over us. Though it still entangles us, the chains have been broken. Sin's tyranny has been vanquished. Jesus set us free!

As new and free creations, our desires change. We have tasted the bitter fruit of sin and been left empty. Now we hunger and thirst for righteousness. We *want* to love God, we *want* to fight temptation, we *want* to grow in godliness. A hunger for holiness isn't the result of legalism; it's the result of having a new heart. We desire to obey God out of loving gratitude for all he's done for us—he's lavished on us grace and kindness, so of course we want to honor him. We desire to overcome corrupted cravings so that we can know his surpassing worth. Our consciences are pricked by sin, precisely because they've been regenerated by the Spirit.

Experiencing conviction over sin should actually encourage rather than condemn us, because it is evidence of being alive in Christ.

It is impossible to be in Christ and *not* have renewed desires. J. I. Packer says it this way: "Regeneration is birth; sanctification is growth. In regeneration, God implants desires that were not there before: desire for God, for holiness, and for the hallowing and glorifying of God's name in the world; desire to pray, worship, love, serve, and please God; desire to show love and bring benefit to others."[14]

Salvation isn't the pinnacle of life in Christ; it's the beginning. After we've been forgiven of our sin and clothed in the righteousness of Christ, the Spirit begins his progressive work of sanctification. Our renewal means we increasingly put to death sexual immorality, impurity, passion, evil desire, covetousness, anger, wrath, malice, slander, obscenity, and lying; and we increasingly put on compassionate hearts, kindness, humility, meekness, patience, forbearance, forgiveness, and love, allowing the peace of Christ to rule in our hearts (Col. 3:1–15).

Far from being a burden, our holy renewal lifts the oppressive bondage of sin—for freedom Christ has set us free (Gal. 5:1).

Freedom Leads to Fruit

We have been grafted into the true vine—Jesus—and the inevitable by-product of abiding in him is spiritual fruit. He said, "I am the vine; you are the branches. Whoever abides in me and I in him, he it is that bears much fruit, for apart from me you can do nothing" (John 15:5).

The fruit of godliness isn't the basis of our reconciliation with God; it is the proof of it. Jesus says, "By this my Father is glorified, that you bear much fruit and so prove to be my disciples" (John 15:8); and, "So, every healthy tree bears good fruit, but the diseased tree bears bad fruit. A healthy tree cannot bear bad fruit, nor can a diseased tree bear good fruit" (Matt. 7:17–18). We simply cannot abide in Christ without bearing good fruit. It is impossible. Freedom always leads to fruit—the fruit of righteousness *and* joy (more on that in chapter 7).

When we come to faith in Christ, our renewed desires result in real change. No longer slaves to selfishness, we begin to serve. No longer slaves to lust, we begin to pursue purity. No longer slaves to greed, we begin to live generously. When the tax collector Zacchaeus encountered Jesus, his faith was immediately evident. He confessed his sins publicly, repaid those he had cheated, and gave half of his goods to the poor. It's not that he was suddenly perfect, but he was sincerely changed. In response, Jesus declared that salvation had come to his house—Zacchaeus's deeds hadn't earned his salvation; they'd proved it.

The only explanation for bearing good fruit is the miracle of a dead branch being grafted into the living vine.

Today, many try to separate love for God from obedience to God. It's a false, and frankly absurd, dichotomy. Jesus is clear that love and obedience go hand in hand: "If you love me, you will keep my commandments" (John 14:15). To *love* God is to *live* for him.

Since love and obedience are inextricably linked, God sent us a helper. The Holy Spirit dwells within all Christians, bearing witness to our salvation *by* empowering us to love and obey God. He is the one who enables you to find contentment when you are tempted to worry or complain about your finances. He is the one who enables you to turn off your computer when you're tempted to view porn, and the TV when you're tempted toward laziness. He is the one who enables you to be kind to your difficult coworker and to love the socially awkward person in your small group. Each time we see evidence of love, joy, peace, patience, kindness, goodness, faithfulness, gentleness, or self-control, we should be encouraged—such fruit testifies to the Spirit at work within us (Gal. 5:22–23).

Ongoing Temptation

No matter how long we've been a Christian, we will always experience temptation. Though I wish I related to a more victorious section of Scripture, I never feel more understood than when I read Paul's conflicted dialogue: "I do not understand my own actions. For I do not do what I want, but I do the very thing I hate. . . . For I know that nothing good dwells in me, that is, in my flesh. For I have the desire to do what is right, but not the ability to carry it out. For I do not do the good I want, but the evil I do not want is what I keep on doing" (Rom. 7:15, 18–19).

It's almost reminiscent of the argument Gollum has in J. R. R. Tolkien's *The Two Towers*, when his two natures—Smeagol (his original identity) and Gollum (his corrupted identity)—are in conflict. Smeagol wants to remain loyal to his new hobbit friends, but the powerful ring is just so alluring to Gollum. He vehemently argues with himself, and we wonder which nature will win.[15]

Because the Spirit indwells us, our nature as sons and daughters of God is certain. Our inner "Gollum" will not prevail. Though it may be unsettling that our sin still rears its ugly head, we must remember that Christ has already defeated Satan and crushed sin's power. Our old self has been crucified with Christ, and the Spirit has raised us in victorious union with him (Gal. 2:19–20).

We are truly reborn, truly remade, and truly redeemed. But we still struggle. Life in Christ doesn't remove temptation. Every day we will experience tension between our old self and old desires and our new self and new desires. We will want to do right, and we will keep doing wrong. We will do what we hate, and not do what we love. And the more we mature in faith, the more aware of our sin we'll become—praise God for his unfailing grace!

This growing awareness of sin may tempt us to despair, but it shouldn't. As God exposes our sin, he is demonstrating his faithfulness. He has united himself to us, and he will tenderly convict us, discipline us, expose us, and strengthen us until we become holy as he is holy.

One of our great frustrations is that we want change to happen overnight. I would love to wake up tomorrow as an unwaveringly patient mother, gracious wife, faithful friend, bold witness, generous giver, and lover of God. One reason I'm so excited for heaven is knowing I won't sin anymore. Can you even imagine? What will it be like to love God and others without even a hint of temptation or speck of sin hindering us? It will be glorious.

Occasionally, God chooses to miraculously free us from specific struggles. While most people wouldn't have guessed it, based on the baggy athletic clothes I wore as a teenager, I struggled with eating disorders for two years. A quick skim through old prayer journals shows what a pervasive idol body image was, and I struggled with being consumed by it. Until one day I wasn't. I hadn't just matured my way out of the battle; God freed me! But low and behold, freedom from that particular sin actually opened up other temptations. Now the temptation to idolize my figure is so foreign that I'm much more likely to be tempted by gluttony, physical laziness, or a judgmental spirit toward those who spend (in my assessment) excessive money or time on their appearance. Fighting sin feels a bit like playing whack-a-mole.

Growth in godliness takes time. There are many means of grace available to help us—prayer, Scripture, fellowship, community—but there aren't any shortcuts or magic pills. To grow in love, our devotion must be tested; to grow in patience, our forbearance must be provoked; to grow in contentment, our joy must be challenged. It is only by weathering trials and temptations that our roots can grow. And many times, in the face of such strains, we will fall. But the Holy Spirit will continually help us. This doesn't mean that our sanctification is always an upward trajectory—Christians can backslide and fall in grievous ways. It means that he is always faithful. He has given us all the defenses we need to fight temptation; we just have to put them on: "Finally, be strong in the Lord and in the strength of his might. Put on the whole armor of God, that you may be able to stand against the schemes of the devil" (Eph. 6:10–11).

Diligent Effort

What do we do with the reality that our regenerated hearts and renewed desires clash with our indwelling sin? Well, we work (Phil. 2:12). We strive (Heb. 12:14). We struggle (Eph. 6:12). We fight (1 Tim. 6:12). We flee (1 Cor. 10:14). We have a responsibility to pursue holiness. If I know I'm tempted by anger, I need to identify ways to fight it. If I know I'm tempted by pride, I need to actively put on humility.

The good news is, we don't have to fight our flesh in the strength of our flesh. Such self-sufficient effort would get us nowhere! Jerry Bridges wrote, "The Holy Spirit works in us to enable us to live lives pleasing to God. He does not do the work for us; rather, He enables us to do the work."[16]

To say we are responsible to strive for holiness is not to negate grace—we only *want* holiness because grace transforms us. And to say we're responsible to strive for holiness is not to negate our dependence—we only *can* strive because the Spirit empowers us (Phil. 2:13).

Scripture's analogy of sowing and reaping is particularly helpful when it comes to grace-empowered effort: "Do not be deceived: God is not mocked, for whatever one sows, that will he also reap. For the one who sows to his own flesh will from the flesh reap corruption, but the one who sows to the Spirit will from the Spirit reap eternal life. And let us not grow weary of doing good, for in due season we will reap, if we do not give up" (Gal. 6:7–9).

A farmer is responsible to till the soil and plant the seeds, but he doesn't actually hold the power to yield a harvest. He cannot control the sun or rain that makes the seeds grow. No matter how hard he works, he remains dependent on UV rays and H_2O for seeds to sprout. In that sense, the farmer is totally dependent. However, if he is lazy in his farming, the crops will suffer. The sun and the rain won't grow the proper vegetation if nobody takes time to till the soil and plant the seeds. In that sense, the farmer is totally responsible.

Likewise, if I make a habit of skipping time in God's word, I shouldn't expect to grow in love for it. If I watch, read, and listen to things that numb my conscience toward sin, I shouldn't expect to grow in discernment. But if I dig into God's word even when it feels dry, I will (eventually) grow a greater love for it. If I watch, read, and listen to things that are true, honorable, just, pure, lovely, commendable, and excellent, I will grow to love what God loves and hate what God hates. Too often, we sow to our flesh and hope to somehow reap godliness anyway. We won't. God will not be mocked.

We must *actively* submit to the Holy Spirit if we are ever to become like the Son. Total dependence enables discipline. We must strive for holiness, remembering that the only reason we even can is because God saved us. Dead farmers can't grow crops, neither can dead sinners bear spiritual fruit. It is only by God's saving grace that we have any hope of being sanctified at all.

Holding onto the Promise

In this life, we will have seasons of growth and seasons of drift. At times, we will clearly recognize the Spirit working in us, empowering us to turn from sin and toward righteousness. Such seasons build our confidence in God's sanctifying grace.

I recently shared with women in my small group ways God has helped me grow in patience toward my children. Since anger is a sin I confess to them often, it was encouraging to recount specific ways God has helped me. It reminded me that I'm not a slave to sin, that he enables me to overcome the temptations that nag me most. We experience similar reassurance of God's enabling grace through fellowship with other Christians. When we are discouraged, it's tempting to doubt our ability to change. But when we see God transforming our brothers and sisters—helping them become more forgiving or generous or self-controlled or kind—it builds our own faith in his ability to change us.

This is an ongoing struggle though. There are times when we are far more aware of the ways we are falling short than ways we are changing. We hear Satan's piercing accusations and wonder if there's even a point to trying when we fail so often. Discouragement is the enemy of repentance. Self-loathing and self-pity only drive us deeper into sin. We must get our gaze off ourselves and onto our Savior!

If we place our hope in our change, our growth, our repentance, or our obedience, we will constantly swing between pride and despair, because we are up and down and all over the place. But Jesus isn't. He is a steadfast foundation. Our longing to change should always point us right back to him—the one who already made us new creations, the one who has already helped us grow, and the one who will finish the good work he started. We will be transformed, because *he* will never forsake the work of his hands.

> When Satan tempts me to despair,
> And tells me of the guilt within,
> Upward I look, and see him there
> Who made an end of all my sin.[17]

Discussion Questions

1. Read Colossians 3:5–15. What specific areas of sin is God calling you to put to death? How can you actively put on the "new self"?

2. Read 2 Corinthians 5:17. How does our union with Christ fuel our repentance and confidence that we can change?

3. In what ways are you being diligent to grow in holiness? In what ways are you being passive?

4. What do you think it would mean for you to be more dependent on the Holy Spirit for growing in godliness?

5. Read Galatians 6:7–9. How is God calling you to sow to the Spirit? What fruit do you hope to reap?

Recommended Reading

Jerry Bridges, *The Fruitful Life* (Colorado Springs, CO: NavPress, 2018).

Hannah Anderson, *Made for More: An Invitation to Live in God's Image* (Chicago, IL: Moody, 2014).

6

Craving Strength

I MARRIED a comic-book nerd and have grown to share his regard for the DC universe. After Batman, Wonder Woman is my favorite superhero. I love her strength and conviction. Her heroism is driven by compassion, justice, and truth, and she uses her power to protect the vulnerable.

It's no wonder I became a fan. *I* want to be strong. A justice doer and a truth seeker. Someone who relentlessly strives to help the vulnerable. A woman who doesn't waver in conviction or struggle with fear but follows Jesus with unflinching faith. I don't want to struggle with limitations or inadequacies or temptations—in other words, I don't want to be weak.

I don't think any of us do.

Oddly enough, it's sometimes easier to confess sin than to expose weakness. There's clarity about how to handle sin. Flee. Resist. Battle. Confess. Repent. Learning to live with our weaknesses is murky. What does dependence actually look like? How do we embrace our God-given limitations without falling into complacency? If faith helps us battle sin, how does it interact with our human frailty?

None of us have enough strength or wisdom. We don't always know the right thing to do and rarely have the capacity to accomplish everything we want (even our most noble and God-honoring aspirations). We stumble. We fail. We grow weary and discouraged and uncertain.

Our weaknesses—though not inherently sinful—also make us vulnerable to temptation, so we need God's help to discern between our need for *dependence* and our need for *repentance*. Yet even when those lines blur, we can have confidence of one thing: our weakness is always a canvas for God's unfailing strength.

In this chapter, we will learn why our limitations are a good thing rather than a problem to overcome. We will also see how our weaknesses are designed to lead us to the very strength we crave, because they lead us to God.

We Are Limited, He Is Not

"You can't do it!" "You are limited!" "Don't aim for the stars—you can barely reach the bottom branch!" There's a reason slogans like these don't become the names of self-help books or motivational conferences. We don't want to accept our limitations. We never have. The serpent tempted Eve by asserting she could become like God (Gen. 3:4–5). The Tower of Babel was erected as a monument to human power and self-reliance (Gen. 11:4). Wars spawn from the insatiable quest for control. Ethical lines are crossed when scientists try to play god. Families fall apart in the futile pursuit to "have it all."

Trying to operate outside of our God-given limitations isn't just innocent optimism or foolish idealism; it's arrogance—an idolatrous attempt to function as if we are God.

When I say I hate being weak, what I'm really saying is that I resent my need for God. I want to be wise and successful *on my own*. I want to conquer sin and follow Christ *on my own*. I want to be so self-sufficient that I'm never forced to seek strength from another source—including God.

As created beings, we are called to embrace our weaknesses, not rail against them. I need rest; I don't know everything; there are countless things I can't control. God is all sufficient, all wise, and all sovereign. It is because of his lovingkindness that we've been created with limits. Life apart from him is dangerous and empty. He wants us close! Our boundary lines keep us dependent. As the source of everything we need, God offers himself to us freely—he *longs* to fill us.

Knowing his desire to fill us also guards us from complacency. While some of us struggle with trying to do too much, others struggle with doing too little. We create little worlds that we can manage in our own strength, never pushing ourselves in ways that require dependence. We don't say yes to what stretches our capacity because we rely on ourselves instead of the Spirit. We don't take risks or challenges because we fear failure and discomfort more than we fear God. Our craving for control, comfort, and security cripples us from wholeheartedly investing our lives for the kingdom. It's heavy to take up a cross—too heavy to do on our own—so we'd rather just leave it behind instead of seeking Christ's help to carry it.

Pursuing lifestyles that are sustainable in our own strength is just as proud as denying our limitations. Rather than trying to guard and preserve what little strength we have, we are called to freely spend it and trust God to replenish us. As Charles Spurgeon once taught, "Give yourself to Christ, and when you have used yourself for His glory, you will be more able to serve Him than you are now. You will find your little supply growing as you spend it."[18]

He Replenishes the Weary

We live in a demanding culture, and it's wearing us out. Chasing unrealistic expectations, we toil day and night as if the fate of the world lies on our shoulders. We'll rest someday, but just not yet. Our children depend on our constant attention. The job promotion is right around the corner. The ministry needs are too important. There is a mile-long checklist to finish first.

If we lack conviction about the importance of rest (in particular, Sabbath rest), we'll begin to live as if rest is an expression of either laziness or luxury rather than a gift from God intended to replenish us.

The sole fact that we need sleep every day shows just how frail we are. Lack of sleep not only affects our mood and concentration; it weakens our immune system and increases our risk of disease.[19] Our bodies *suffer* from sleeplessness. This is an expression of God's mercy to us. Knowing our bent toward self-sufficiency, he has imbedded us with a need that operates as a daily alarm, reminding us that we are *not* him. We need sleep. And the world will keep spinning while we do, because he's the one running it.

Outside of daily needs, there are times when our physical weaknesses amplify. Pregnancy is a reminder of God's amazing design of the female body, as well as the limitations of it. While I was pregnant, the relentless exhaustion and nausea were overwhelming. Despite loving my job, work became a burden. Cooking dinner became unthinkable. And hormonal emotions were, well, uncontrollable. I was so weak.

Those with long-lasting illnesses feel their physical weakness even more acutely. My brother has Crohn's disease, and his many hospitalizations and surgeries over the years have impacted his family life and work as a pastor. He is a go-getter, naturally bent toward productivity, and his disease has slowed him down and created boundary lines he never would have chosen.

Whether our physical weakness is due to something as serious as cancer or simply a sleepless night with a newborn, it feels like a hindrance to faithfulness. Surely we'd serve God better if we were energized and healthy! On a human level, it certainly seems this way. But we only have a partial perspective. Just think of Joni Eareckson Tada. Joni has spent more than fifty years as a quadriplegic, suffering weakness that most of us can't imagine. And yet God has used her—not despite her limitations but *through* them—to minister to countless people.

The God drawing our boundary lines knows exactly which ones we need. He never draws them haphazardly. He is carefully working to accomplish a plan designed to sanctify us and serve his mission. Sometimes it may feel like he's put us on the sidelines, and we just don't understand why. But in team sports, players are put on the sidelines for a reason. It's so they can recoup and others can get in the game. When we are exhausted and sent to the bench, it's God's way of reminding us that we are just one player on the team. He doesn't depend on us. He's already got the game plan, and he knows when to use us and when to give us a breather. We can trust him. We can rest.

He Lifts Up the Humble

I have always been an extremely forgetful and disorganized person. I rarely leave the house without returning moments later for something left behind. I always end up buying gifts on the way to baby showers and weddings. And my family will never let me live down how I accidentally missed my niece's first birthday party—my brother even called to see where I was, but I'd gone for a long walk and forgotten my phone (of course). Sometimes my forgetfulness gives others ripe material for banter, and it's easy to laugh about. Other times, it leaves me feeling incompetent, irresponsible, or uncaring because of how it affects others.

If I've been like this all my life, chances are I'll stay this way. Embracing this weakness doesn't mean taking a passive attitude because, *oh well, it's just who I am*. Rather, it's realizing that *because* this is how I am, I need God's help.

Recently, a friend shared with me a way I had hurt her. She had experienced a sudden loss, and I'd offered to get together. But I failed to follow up until several days later, and by that point, her most intense wave of grief had already subsided. My neglect wasn't due to being mean-spirited; I just forgot. That didn't make my actions any less hurtful. Thankfully she was gracious enough to talk to me about it rather than bearing a grudge, which gave me the opportunity to apologize.

How often, though, do we choose the road of pride when we should just admit to how our weaknesses affect others? Usually, our instinct is to defend our motives instead of humbly apologizing.

Regardless of our gifting or disposition, we all have weaknesses. Though they may not necessarily be rooted in sin, it is arrogant to dismiss their impact on others. We are called to take responsibility and apologize when our actions affect others, even if our intent wasn't sinful. We can also trust that when we do mess up, God is near. Others may groan in frustration over our shortcomings, but he doesn't. His heart is filled with a gentle desire to come alongside and help us.

Ironically, our weaknesses often exist on the flipside of our strengths. This is important to keep in mind. Someone naturally organized and administrative might have a tendency to micromanage others. Someone who is a natural leader and go-getter might inadvertently plow over others. Someone who is thoughtful and discerning and *not* domineering might frustrate others by being a slow or indecisive decision-maker. This tension reminds us that we *always* need God's help. Even at our best, we are wholly dependent beings. Just as we shouldn't despair over our shortcomings, we shouldn't take pride in our strengths. Rather, we must turn from self-reliance altogether and live in humble dependence on God.

He Encourages the Fainthearted

Not only do we experience physical weakness and limitations, but we have emotional struggles too. God created us with minds and hearts that *feel*. Our emotions are a gift that have been touched by the fall. We experience anger, anxiety, and despair. Some of us have depression or post-traumatic stress disorder (PTSD). Navigating our emotions is confusing because of how often sin and weakness overlap. Hidden and habitual sin, discontentment, and spiritual laziness can all contribute to depression; so can hormones and trauma.

When it comes to seeking God's strength through our emotional and mental weaknesses, it's helpful to have a nuanced—rather than either/or—mentality. God's word is our daily bread, so we *need* to be anchored in truth when suffering depression. But he's provided the gift of medicine too. For some, taking antidepressants is an expression of faithful dependence. God is also powerful enough to heal those suffering from PTSD or anxiety disorders. But he works through counselors and psychiatrists too. We need not spurn the grace he provides to help us.

Where theology is valued, we often worry that discussing things like mental illness or trauma or chemical imbalances will lead to excuses for sin. It's a fair concern. Pop psychology has undoubtedly been misused for that purpose. Yet if the whole world aches with brokenness, should we resist the thought that our *brains* bear scars of brokenness too? Seeing the reality of both also helps us view God in a greater light. He is the redeemer of sinful souls *and* the restorer of broken bodies. He not only offers refuge to the repentant, but to the brokenhearted, the fearful, and the afflicted.

I have worked with children with developmental needs for over fifteen years, and some of them had co-occurring anxiety disorders. In an effort to understand their struggles, I read several books on brain development and listened to dozens of lectures by neuroscientists and experts in the fields of psychology. The complex nature of the brain is just astounding. While scientists used to believe that our brains are hardwired, modern research shows that they are actually elastic. On the one hand, this is encouraging. It means that our brains can heal and forge new and healthier pathways. On the other hand, it means that trauma and persistent stress or fear can harm our brains more easily than previously thought. This research drastically altered my approach to helping the children I worked with. It also has profound implications for the way we care for *anyone* in distress.

It is this premise that separates a good counselor from a bad one (whether the counselor is a pastor, a professional, or a friend). Wise counselors seek to understand us—our backgrounds, our experiences, our struggles, our diagnoses—*so that* they can best apply God's word to us. Scripture remains the ultimate authority, but understanding the *why* behind someone's struggle helps us apply truth in ways that take her weaknesses into account. Some people need to be admonished; others simply need to be helped and encouraged (1 Thess. 5:14).

This is how God treats us. He doesn't demand that we suppress our emotions and get in line. He is gentle. His heart is tender toward us. He aches to bring peace to our anxieties. He draws close in our despair. He invites us to approach him *in* our weakness so that we can be held by *his* strong arms. Forcing a stiff upper lip doesn't draw us closer to God. Weakness does. Weakness makes us look for the help he is eager to provide.

My daughter has a mild seizure disorder, and the side effect of one medication we tried was vivid nightmares. For several sleepless nights she spent hours convinced that a snake was on her arm trying to bite her. Even though I stayed in her bed and held her close as I prayed over her, she couldn't stop shaking and screaming. I wasn't frustrated by her irrational fear; I was grieved by her distress and wanted nothing more than to bring her comfort.

God's heart is even softer toward us. He sees us in our weakness, and regardless of *why* we're struggling, he longs to comfort us. He *wants* to be our refuge. He *wants* us to turn to him for strength and comfort and peace. He doesn't want us to face our struggles and fight them on our own—he wants us to rush to him. To cling to him. To cry into his arms. To let him wipe our tears. His heart aches to help us.

He Delivers Us from Evil

Finally—and perhaps most of all—we feel our weakness and desperate need for God when we are tempted. Many of our temptations are born from our own evil desires (James 1:13), and the more we give in to them, the harder they are to resist. In this way, we contribute—at least in part—to the temptations we face. The inclination toward evil is *within* us. This is why it's so crucial for us to grow in discernment, lest our own foolishness lead us into temptation. A recovering alcoholic doesn't walk alone into a bar and assume she'll be fine; she avoids the bar altogether. That's not legalism—it's wisdom.

At the same time, it's important to realize that being tempted is not a sin. Even Jesus was tempted. When he took on humanity, he shared in all of our weaknesses—physical, emotional, *and* spiritual. To this point, there are a few vital distinctions to make. Unlike us, Jesus wasn't born with a sinful nature. Unlike us, Jesus never battled his own depravity or indwelling sin. He was and is completely holy. However, to conquer sin, it was necessary that he be tempted by it. He is even more acquainted with temptation than we are—in order to overcome to the uttermost, he was tempted to the uttermost. "For we do not have a high priest who is unable to sympathize with our weaknesses, but one who *in every respect* has been tempted as we are, yet without sin" (Heb. 4:15).

Feeling our weakness in the face of temptation shouldn't cause us to hide away in shame. We might wish that temptations toward laziness and lust would lose their appeal. We might wish that we aren't tempted to fear man or worry about the future. We just want to love God with all our hearts and never feel enticed by our flesh again. Yet our spiritual weakness is meant to drive us to Christ, who fully understands and conquered temptation. "Let us then with confidence draw near to the throne of grace, that we may receive mercy and find grace to help in time of need" (Heb. 4:16).

God graciously liberates us from the appeal of many evils. However, it's a mistake to believe that lack of temptation is necessarily a sign of spiritual maturity. God's mercy might be most evident when he frees us from specific sins, but his *strength* is most evident when he empowers us to fight them. It's easy to be at peace when you aren't provoked. Anyone can do that. But when the temptation to lash out burns in your chest and you know your only hope is to cry out to God, *that* is evidence that God is helping you depend on his strength rather than your own.

Pride prowls like a lion when we don't sense our spiritual need. It's one of Satan's greatest tactics. We gain a false sense of safety, imagining ourselves too mature or godly to be overpowered. This lures us away from our greatest source of protection: dependence on Christ. This is why he instructed us to pray, "Lead us not into temptation, but deliver us from evil" (Matt. 6:13).

Willpower alone is too fragile to fight temptation. Recognizing our spiritual weakness keeps us close to God, who delivers us from evil. We aren't strong enough. He is. Take heart: "No temptation has overtaken you that is not common to man. God is faithful, and he will not let you be tempted beyond your ability, *but with the temptation he will also provide the way of escape, that you may be able to endure it"* (1 Cor. 10:13).

A Strength That Never Runs Out

One reason we struggle to seek God's strength is that we project our own tendencies onto him. We know the frustration of dealing with someone else's weaknesses. We grow weary of helping the needy child or the needy coworker or the needy friend. Since we ourselves are limited, we are limited in our ability to help others. We eventually burn out.

Not so with God.

God is never resistant to our pleas for help. He never turns us away, fed up that we're coming in weakness once again. He never tells us to buck up and get over it. Unlike the exhausted mom who hides in the bathroom and desperately prays her toddler will allow her just one minute alone, God never hides from us. So great is his strength that he is never drained or weary.

God's posture toward us is always one of welcome. When we are tempted and need help, he welcomes us. When we are perplexed and need wisdom, he welcomes us. When we are discouraged and need reassurance, he welcomes us. When we are tired and need a resting place, he welcomes us. He refuses to send us away. He refuses to withhold his strengthening grace. We are never left to fend for ourselves, because his heart is bent on helping us. He is the endless reserve of the strength we crave, and he will pour it out to us generously if we ask.

Don't be timid about your need. Don't pretend you are stronger than you are. We may successfully mask our weaknesses before others, but God isn't fooled by brave faces. We are fully exposed before him. There is no need to hide—his power is made perfect in weakness.

> For I will satisfy the weary soul, and every languishing soul I will replenish. (Jer. 31:25)

Discussion Questions

1. Is it difficult for you to admit areas of weakness? Why or why not?

2. Are you more tempted to try living outside of your limitations (as if you were God) or to stay within your comfort zone (so that you don't feel your need for God)? How can you pursue a more God-dependent life?

3. Read 2 Corinthians 12:7–10. What does it mean to "boast" in weakness? How does God use our weaknesses to manifest his strength and power?

4. What weaknesses most impact your daily life? How can you seek God—and others—for help?

5. Read Hebrews 4:15–16. Christ not only sympathizes with our weaknesses; he also understands and overcame every temptation. How does this truth help you approach his throne of grace with confidence to receive help in time of need?

6. How have you experienced God's strength in the face of weariness, discouragement, or temptation? What Scripture verses have been a comfort to you?

Recommended Reading

Trillia Newbell, *Sacred Endurance: Finding Grace and Strength for a Lasting Faith* (Westmont, IL: InterVarsity Press, 2019).

J. I. Packer, *Weakness Is the Way: Life with Christ Our Strength* (Wheaton, IL: Crossway, 2013).

7

Craving Happiness

"EVERY MAN, whatsoever his condition, desires to be happy."[20] First-century African theologian Saint Augustine aptly captured a universal truth: a hunger for happiness is deeply entrenched in every heart. So great is this longing that it was penned into the Declaration of Independence: "We hold these truths to be self-evident, that all men are created equal, that they are endowed by their Creator with certain unalienable Rights, that among these are Life, Liberty and the pursuit of Happiness." What a beautiful statement to mark the birth of a country—if only it had been equally applied to all people!

A desire for happiness is at the core of our decision-making, big and small. This quest influences whether we eat ice cream or kale, whether we are social or reclusive, whether we have children or pets, whether we work or rest. No matter what we pursue or how we pursue it, our fundamental goal is the same. The overachiever and the sloth, the shopaholic and the penny pincher, the partier and the homebody, are all driven by what they think will make them happy.

There is a reason for this impulse. In this chapter we'll see that God created us with an instinctual desire for happiness because he is a happy God. The Father, Son, and Spirit eternally delight in one another, and in kindness God invites his creatures to share in his joy. He *wants* us to be happy. And when we actually believe this, it helps us walk in holiness and enjoy his good gifts, trusting that our Father smiles upon us.

God Is Happy

When I consider the nature of God, what usually comes to mind are words like *holy, sovereign, powerful, righteous, glorious, merciful, just*, and *loving*. I rarely think of him as *happy*. It seems too carnal—almost as if happiness is beneath him. Yet our eternally existing God is happy. He delights in himself. He delights in his work. And he delights in us.

The three persons of the Trinity—Father, Son, and Spirit—enjoy unceasing happiness in one another. After Jesus was baptized by John, the Spirit of God descended and declared, "This is my beloved Son, with whom I am well pleased" (Matt. 3:17).

That moment in time echoed an eternal truth. God is always pleased—that is, happy, content, delighted, and satisfied—in himself. We may struggle with this concept because it seems tinged with pride, and if anyone else said it, it would be. But as the endless spring of goodness and glory and grace, of course God is happy! While our happiness ebbs and flows based on its source, God *is* the source. As such, his happiness never ceases.

The entire universe was created out of God's good pleasure. He certainly didn't need it. He wasn't bored or unfulfilled or lonely. Creation was an overflow of his generous spirit to share himself and his happiness with us. Every detail—from the towering oak to the trickling stream—drips with his delight. Everything he made was good.

When sin marred creation, God didn't scrap the whole thing and start over. Instead, he chose to redeem and restore the world because he delights in it. Consider the wonder of that reality—God would rather rescue wicked rebels and make us new than start over with someone new. It was "for the joy that was set before him" that Jesus went to the cross (Heb. 12:2), so that someday he will "present you blameless before the presence of his glory with great joy" (Jude 24).

God is *happy* to save us. Jesus emphasized this repeatedly through his parables. When the lost sheep was found, the shepherd rejoiced and invited others to celebrate with him (Luke 15:4–7). When the lost coin was found, the woman rejoiced and invited others to celebrate with her (Luke 15:8–10). When the Prodigal Son returned, the father ran to him, kissed and embraced him, and threw a party to celebrate (Luke 15:11–32). In the same way, God's happiness over rescued sinners is so great that he cannot resist inviting others to join the celebration; his cheer is the loudest among the heavenly chorus when a prodigal comes home.

Barriers to Happiness

The pursuit of happiness was *supposed* to be a good thing, but then sin entered the world and turned it all upside down. Ever since Genesis 3, the godly pursuit of happiness has been obstructed by sin. Eve plucked the forbidden fruit because of unbelief. Rather than trusting that her greatest happiness was found in God, she imagined he was withholding good from her—surely she'd be happier if she took matters into her own hands.

It is our distrust of God, *not* our desire for happiness, that leads to disobedience. If we believe God is a taker rather than a giver, we won't trust that his law is an expression of his love. If we believe he is withholding good, it is far easier to taste the forbidden. It's why we turn to sins like gluttony, sexual immorality, and greed. The pleasure is right there at our fingertips, so close we can almost taste it. Instead of trusting God's warnings, we are enticed by warped desires. It never pays off. Though sin is enjoyable for a time, it always leaves us miserable.

Another barrier to happiness is idolatry. Though idolatry is occasionally rooted in explicitly sinful desires, it is usually rooted in disordered ones. It's good for me to love my husband. However, if he becomes an idol—someone I look to as the *source* of my happiness and peace—I will end up unhappy. No matter how good of a husband he is (and he's a great one), he is a pitiful substitute for God. The same could be said of our jobs and friendships and possessions and homes. Loving gifts more than the giver chips away at our happiness with both. Little by little, we grow discontented when our idols don't deliver. And how could they? Only when we keep good gifts in their proper place can we fully enjoy them.

Entitlement and ingratitude are also common thieves of happiness. Research indicates that there is "little correlation between the circumstances of people's lives and how happy they are,"[21] and that the practice of gratitude increases happiness.[22] This, of course, doesn't mean that our emotions won't fluctuate or that grief is avoidable. It does, however, indicate that our circumstances have less to do with happiness than we assume. The rich aren't necessarily happier than the poor; the comfortable aren't necessarily happier than the suffering. So it would seem that much of our unhappiness is rooted in discontentment. If we believe God owes us a certain set of circumstances, we will overlook the spiritual and physical blessings we *have* received and resent not having more. We will groan and whine like the Israelites, never satisfied with God's provision. We will walk through life like the Prodigal Son—valuing our inheritance more than our Father.

Sin is absolutely toxic to joy. Anytime we walk in patterns of disobedience, idolatry, ingratitude, or entitlement, we shouldn't be surprised by the bitter fruit of unhappiness.

This is not to say that *all* unhappiness is caused by sin. We live in a broken world, and grief and pain will paint our days until we are ushered into heaven. The fight for happiness can't be won by stifling sorrow or positive pep talks. Learning to lament before God is vital to our spiritual health (more on this in the following chapter). No loving father wants his children to hide their suffering—God wants to comfort us. As the healer of the brokenhearted, he cares when our hearts are left in pieces.

Does God Want Us Holy or Happy? Yes.

There is a popular Christian adage that goes something like this: "God is concerned about your holiness, not your happiness." I've said it myself. At first glance, it seems like a spiritually mature sentiment. The problem is, it creates a false dichotomy. God is actually *very* passionate about our happiness. Holiness and happiness were never intended to be pitted against each other. On the contrary, growth in holiness *increases* happiness.

It's also important to consider the implications of this message: to believe that holiness involves the sacrifice of happiness is to deny the goodness of God's law. Such denial dishonors God. Submitting to his commandments, statutes, and rule should bring us delight. In the psalms we see this repeatedly, particularly in Psalm 119:

> In the way of your testimonies I delight
> > as much as in all riches. . . .
> Lead me in the path of your commandments,
> > for I delight in it. . . .
> My soul keeps your testimonies;
> > I love them exceedingly. (vv. 14, 35, 167)

Following God doesn't dissipate joy; it fuels it.

This, of course, doesn't mean the pursuit of holiness won't involve sacrifice. Crucifying our flesh is painful. It is easier to indulge greed than to fight it. It is easier to have a loose tongue than to bridle it. It is easier to feed bitterness than to absorb the cost of forgiveness. There are pleasures we may want but of which we cannot partake, and our self-denial will hurt at times. However, none of this means God calls us to sacrifice happiness for the sake of holiness. Though in the moment of temptation it *feels* as if we must choose between the two, we will ultimately find that every choice to pursue holiness results in more happiness, not less.

When I consider the fleeting joy of indulging sin, it is nothing compared to the sweeter happiness of following Christ. Giving money away always leaves me happier than hoarding it. Biting my tongue always leaves me happier than the sting of regret over rash words. Using my time to serve others always leaves me happier than being self-consumed. Engaging in spiritual disciplines always leaves me happier than neglecting them. This fruit of happiness is rarely immediate though. Walking in obedience is uncomfortable and, at times, even painful. Sin, on the other hand, provides immediate pleasure or relief to our cravings. When I'm in an argument with someone, it feels good to vent my anger and use my words as weapons. When I'm not in the mood to help my neighbor, it feels good to ignore her text and watch TV. However, since true happiness is found in Christ, habits of disobedience *eventually* lead to deeper misery, while habits of holiness ultimately lead to deeper happiness.

Culture preaches that nothing is worse than denying our desires—it's the cardinal sin of our age. But Jesus said, "If anyone would come after me, let him deny himself and take up his cross daily and follow me. For whoever would save his life will lose it, but whoever loses his life for my sake will save it" (Luke 9:23–24). Denying ourselves and taking up our cross *daily* is the only way to follow Jesus and thus the only way to happiness.

Once, a rich young man asked Jesus how to inherit eternal life. By all appearances, the man had committed himself to a morally blameless life. Yet Jesus saw that his heart was enslaved—he was a worshiper of wealth. Moved with love, Jesus said, "You lack one thing: go, sell all that you have and give to the poor, and you will have treasure in heaven; and come, follow me." Unable to see the greater worth of Jesus, the man walked away sad (Mark 10:17–22).

Following Jesus costs everything, yet it offers infinitely more. It is giving up our vain obsession with appearance for the *greater* beauty of Christ. It is giving up sexual impurity—even if that entails a life of celibacy—for the *greater* intimacy of knowing

God. It is giving up power and fame for the *greater* glory of being called children of the Father. It is striving after love, peace, kindness, and goodness for the *greater* reward of life in the Spirit. If we, like the rich young ruler, weigh the cost of discipleship and turn away sad, it is only because we haven't understood Jesus's true worth. The call to holiness isn't a weight to languish under but an invitation that propels us toward true happiness. Nothing we sacrifice compares to the joy of knowing Jesus.

Charlies Spurgeon once said, "Let us show to the people of the world, who think our religion to be slavery, that it is to us a delight and a joy! Let our gladness proclaim that we serve a good Master."[23] Our desire for happiness isn't an impulse to put to death; it is one to embrace. It drives us to Christ, helps us fight temptation, and bears testimony to the world of our Savior's surpassing worth.

Enjoying God's Good Gifts

God is generous, and the whole earth is filled with his gifts. He delights to display his glory, and he loves to delight *us*. He gave us taste buds so that we could enjoy the sweetness of chocolate. He gave us eyes to behold the beauty of earth, sky, and sea. He gave us ears to be enraptured by soft melodies and thrilling crescendos. Think of all the joy derived from touch—from the intimate pleasures of sex to the unbridled joy of a child being tickled. Even long hugs increase our oxytocin—the "happy hormone"—levels.

God didn't have to make us this way. He could have just created us with senses that enable us to survive. Instead, he chose to design us with senses that enable us to *enjoy*. He wants us to receive his generous gifts with gladness.

Sometimes these gifts make us burst with happiness. We never forget the joy we felt when a beloved family member turned to Christ for salvation, or when we first held our child after a painful birth or adoption process, or when the doctor reported that the cancer was gone, or when God miraculously provided for an urgent need. Sometimes our joy is so full that we overflow in tears.

We also experience countless moments of unremarkable happiness—meals enjoyed with friends, rainy Saturday mornings cuddled in front of the TV, getting lost in a good book, eating tacos, going swimming, laughing at a hilarious meme. Just think about your week—God has filled it with ordinary gifts for you to enjoy.

It is only because *God* bestowed his goodness upon us that we cherish the gifts of friendship and laughter, that we enjoy the fun of games and competitions, that we know the happiness of exploring new places and the gladness of coming home. It is only because of God's abundant kindness that we celebrate marriages and births and holidays and traditions. We dance and feast and heartily apply *his* instruction: "Go, eat your bread with joy, and drink your wine with a merry heart, for God has already approved what you do" (Eccles. 9:7).

Partaking in such pleasure honors God. The happiness he offers extends past Bible study and corporate worship into the ordinary days of our ordinary lives, where we have the privilege of receiving and enjoying and sharing his good gifts.

Feel God's Pleasure

In the Oscar-winning historical drama *Chariots of Fire*, Olympian runner Eric Liddell says, "When I run, I feel His pleasure."[24] I have often felt the same way about writing, not only when I write Christ-centered content, but also when I write fiction and poetry. It doesn't matter that my words might never leave my computer or serve any spiritual purpose; I feel God's pleasure when I write them. Maybe you feel the same way when you sing, teach, paint, garden, cook, or ski.

God isn't a utilitarian who takes pleasure in us only for what we can produce for his kingdom—he takes pleasure in us for simply *being* who he has created us to be. He has woven us together in intricate detail, giving us specific talents and interests and passions for no other reason than it was his good will to do so. Just like a loving father cheers from the bleachers when his daughter nails the soccer move she's been practicing, God smiles from heaven as he watches us exercise the talents he's given us.

It is tempting to create articifial realms between the spiritual and the unspiritual, as if God is pleased only when we pray, evangelize, read our Bibles, or serve at church. Though these spiritual disciplines are vital, they are not the *full* picture of Christian life. And if we don't see God's presence in every sphere of our lives, we will overlook enjoying the fullness we have in him.

God is pleased when we love and obey him, but he also delights in our delight. Once we've been united to Christ, our happiness becomes his too. So closely does he identify with our joy that his heart beats in tandem with ours. When he turns our mourning into dancing, he dances along with us.

When I was a kid, I loved collecting tchotchkes. The dollar store was a wonderland to find cheap figurines and ever-so-classy crystal decorations for my bedroom. My mom, who is remarkably organized and adverse to clutter, didn't understand the appeal of these little treasures. But because she loved *me*, she'd happily wrap them up at Christmas and enjoy watching my "oohs" and "ahhs" when I opened them.

We take joy in seeing the joy of those we love. And the more we love them, the more our happiness rises with theirs. When a son or daughter receives a diploma, we cheer louder than when a classmate does. When a close friend lands the job or runs the marathon or gets married, we don't celebrate primarily because we're happy for ourselves; we celebrate because we're happy for her.

If God loves us more deeply than anyone else in the universe does, we can be assured that he delights in us too.

Unfading Happiness

The happiness we experience now is only a shadow of what's to come. Heaven is not some ethereal place full of melodious harps and floating clouds. Nor is it merely an improved version of our present world. It is a place so supremely joyful it will burst endlessly with roars of praise. A soft melody could never contain our excitement.

We will get to explore the new heavens and the new earth, enjoying God's creation without the polluting effects of sin. We will do fulfilling work without the pain of thorns or thistles. We will learn and discover and enjoy. We will cherish perfectly loving and harmonious relationships.

Above all, we will adore. Finally face-to-face with Christ, our joy will overflow. We will finally see how his mysterious plan really was good, and how he used our hardship to deepen our happiness. We will finally know how deeply loved we are and how incomparably wonderful he is. We will stand in awe of his forgiveness and grace and mercy and goodness toward us.

Now we see in part. Now the joy we experience is only a flicker of what's to come. Then we will see fully. Our happiness will no longer wax and wane like a moon in its orbit; it will burn as brightly as the sun because it exists forever in the Son.

As there is the most heat nearest to the sun, so there is the most happiness nearest to Christ.[25]

Discussion Questions

1. Do you think of God as happy? Why or why not?

2. In what ways have you been tempted to pit happiness against holiness? How does a belief in the goodness of God confront this false dichotomy?

3. Read Psalm 119:35. Do you tend to see God's commands as good or burdensome? Why?

4. Read the story of the rich young ruler (Mark 10:17–22). In what ways has following Jesus cost you something? How has the happiness of knowing him outweighed that sacrifice?

5. The word *blessed* could also be translated as "happy." Read the beatitudes (Matt. 5:2–11), replacing "blessed" with the word *happy*. How does that change your understanding of Jesus's sermon?

Recommended Reading

Randy Alcorn, *Happiness* (Carol Stream, IL: Tyndale, 2015).

Barnabas Piper, *Hoping for Happiness: Turning Life's Most Elusive Feeling into Lasting Reality* (Charlotte, NC: Good Book Company, 2020).

8

Craving Comfort

"IN THE BEGINNING, God created the heavens and the earth" (Gen. 1:1). God formed a perfect world and declared that it was good. Amidst a beautiful garden lived his crowning glory, Adam and Eve, the only creatures honored to be image bearers of the Almighty. They dwelt in perfect peace, working to subdue the earth without the pain of thorns or thistles. If only the story ended there.

Foreshadowing the sin that would plague generations to come, Adam and Eve indulged unbelief. Doubting the goodness of their Creator and rebelliously asserting their will above his, they ate from the tree of the knowledge of good and evil. The result was devastating. As their teeth broke through the skin of the fruit, the world broke too; as they tasted the forbidden, they ensured we would taste suffering.

Now, despite the immeasurable mercies God bestows over creation, our fallen world promises pain. Sometimes we suffer because of sin (both ours and others'), and sometimes we suffer because of natural causes—pandemics, diseases, hurricanes—which really aren't natural at all, but rather the result of a fallen world. We are guarded by neither wealth nor education, location or family ties. Even the deepest faith cannot insulate us from feeling the impact of the fall. So along with the rest of creation, we groan and long for redemption (Rom. 8:22–23). Along with the rest of creation, we need comfort.

The good news is that Jesus entered into our suffering and will ultimately prevail over it. His death and resurrection didn't just secure the forgiveness of our sins; they sealed the promise that he will someday restore and redeem everything that's been broken (Rev. 21:1–5). In the meantime, he warns that we'll have tribulation in this world, yet he encourages us to take heart because he has overcome it (John 16:33). It is vital—for our faith and fruitfulness—to take his words to heart.

In this chapter, we will consider the reality of suffering and the refuge of Christ. Though he prepares us to weep and lament, he promises to turn our sorrow into unshakable joy (John 16:20–22). We have every reason to hope. As we cry out for comfort, our Savior is filled with compassion. He is near, he is listening, and someday he will deliver us.

Even a Good Life Is Hard

I used to think that most Christians in first-world countries didn't know much about suffering and that their difficult circumstances could primarily be considered first-world problems. Meaning, not very serious. There were outliers, of course—those suffering because of cancer or abuse or infidelity. But in arrogance I believed that *most* churches—including my own—were filled with people who didn't know what real suffering was. After all, even those with financial pressure had places to live and food to eat. Even those with medical needs had access to good health care. Nobody sitting down the row from me was a victim of human trafficking or persecution—"real" suffering. I chalked most pain up to a problem in perspective.

There is a morsel of truth there. Many of us engage in sinful habits of complaint, resenting God for what he has withheld rather than giving thanks for what he has provided. We should keep our hearts in check: Is our house really too small? Are we really suffering when we feel unfulfilled at our jobs? Do the religious pressures we face really equate to persecution? Many of us feed discontentment with our entitled longings, but practicing gratitude in our own lives—*and* cultivating compassion for those facing poverty and oppression—will help keep first-world problems in perspective.

However, though some of our troubles spawn from our own sins of selfishness and discontentment, real suffering touches us all. Even a good life is hard. Even if we have grown up in loving families, even if we don't struggle with mental illness, even if we are physically healthy, even if we have decent jobs, even if we don't face financial pressure, living in a fallen world fills our lives with tears. A strong marriage can still endure devastating pain. A wealthy family can still suffer sudden loss. A healthy church can still endure challenges, divisions, and trials that rock it to its core. If life hasn't felt hard for us yet, we probably just haven't lived long enough.

Suffering people fill our pews and attend our small groups and serve in our church ministries. On the surface, life might appear good. Upon closer inspection, many of them have experienced profound pain. I think of friends who enjoy some semblance of privilege and prosperity and yet have walked through nightmares. They have fathers who abandoned them and siblings who are entangled in addiction. They have suffered infertility, miscarriages, and stillborn babies. They have been shattered by infidelity. They have lost loved ones to accidents, sicknesses, and suicide. They have chronic illnesses. They have sat with their children through chemo treatments. Their obedience to God has resulted in scorn from their families and isolation in their workplaces. They have been victims of domestic violence. They have been sexually abused. They have said goodbye to foster children they adored. Their hearts have been broken by the prodigals they love.

During a season when my family was thriving, and exciting endeavors were coming to fruition, my life was rocked with a shocking hit—the kind that knocks the wind out of you. Isn't that so often how it goes? We are just walking through life as usual, when disaster strikes and leaves us in a mess of heaving sobs. It could be a diagnosis or a death or a betrayal or a loss—whatever it is, we weren't ready. It blindsides us. The situation explodes like a grenade, and we can do nothing but watch in horror as the shrapnel pierces us and the people we love most. Whatever blessings we still possess don't soften the intensity of the pain we feel.

When our lives have been predominately "good," it is this kind of suffering that staggers us. We are familiar with disappointment and heartache, not devastation! Regardless of the gifts we've received from God, the circumstances causing us pain can be completely overwhelming. No one escapes the crushing grip of suffering that chokes our hope so violently that we echo the psalmist: "I am weary with my moaning; every night I flood my bed with tears; I drench my couch with my weeping" (Ps. 6:6). But should we be surprised that our hearts ache and our tears flow, when the Savior we follow was called "a man of sorrows" (Isa. 53:3)?

Suffering with Christ

Historically and globally, Christians have been sufferers. Yet most modern Christians in the West have enjoyed substantial religious freedom and very little faith-related suffering. We don't have to hide our Bibles. We freely attend church. We have unhindered access to books on theology and doctrine. We can tell others about the hope we have in Christ without fear of retribution. We have much to be grateful for—these are astounding blessings.

And yet because we are so accustomed to these comforts, we have grown to expect them. This expectation leaves us rattled when we—or other Christians—are opposed for our faith, even though John warned, "Do not be surprised, brothers, that the world hates you" (1 John 3:13). Our hearts enflame at the injustice, even though Jesus said, "Remember the word that I said to you: 'A servant is not greater than his master.' If they persecuted me, they will also persecute you" (John 15:20).

We must be prepared. As Western culture grows increasingly hostile to Christianity, our hope isn't found in fighting for political power or reclaiming the "moral majority." Though Christians can faithfully engage our politics and culture, these are limited means to limited ends. As Jesus showed Peter on the mount of Gethsemane, the kingdom wouldn't come by force (Matt. 26:41–54). Jesus would win through sacrifice, not a sword. And the church must remember this today. Our hope is not in government or society. It's in God. We will assuredly be tested, but if we share in Christ's suffering we will also be blessed. Peter encourages, "Beloved, do not be surprised at the fiery trial when it comes upon you to test you, as though something strange were happening to you. But rejoice insofar as you share Christ's sufferings, that you may also rejoice and be glad when his glory is revealed. If you are insulted for the name of Christ, you are blessed, because the Spirit of glory and of God rests upon you" (1 Pet. 4:12–14).

If we try to shield ourselves from suffering for Christ, we will not live as faithful witnesses to the world. However, if we preach Christ and him crucified, we will be scorned. If we hold fast to sound doctrine, we will be judged by those who compromise it. If we deny our flesh to obey God, it will cost us. It is no easy task to walk in integrity when others manipulate, to love our enemies when they mistreat us, or to fight temptation in a world that celebrates sin. But we can face such suffering in faith, agreeing with Paul: "So we do not lose heart. Though our outer self is wasting away, our inner self is being renewed day by day. For this light momentary affliction is preparing for us an eternal weight of glory beyond all comparison" (2 Cor. 4:16–17).

Our affliction doesn't seem light and momentary when we're in it. But when we consider the eternal glory awaiting us, it strengthens us to stand firm and hold fast.

Be patient in your suffering. Victory is coming.

Our Pain Needs Comfort

When we are hit with suffering of all kinds, we find ourselves desperate for comfort. And we won't find it in shallow platitudes or empty promises. God offers comfort in many ways, but he primarily comforts us through his word and through his people.

The more we know God's word, the more we know *him*. And the more we know him, the more we find him to be everything he promises. He is a father to the forsaken and forgotten. He is a refuge for those in distress. He is a healer of the brokenhearted and a defender of the oppressed. And *he* is the one who turns our mourning into joy.

Penned throughout Scripture, we see story after story of God's sovereign hands at work. Sure and steady, he directs human history to fulfill his redemptive plan. When Joseph is sold into slavery and Esther is taken to a king's harem, God's unseen hand is orchestrating it all. When it seems like evil wins, his justice reigns. When all seems hopeless, his promises prove true. He is a good and trustworthy God. When we saturate ourselves in Scripture, the faithfulness God displayed *then* strengthens us to trust him *now*.

We are a forgetful people. God carries us through countless trials, and yet suffering still tempts us to doubt his sovereignty. We have seen him work all things for good before, but when we can't imagine any possible road to redemption, we wonder if he got it wrong this time. When Asaph's soul was in despair, weary from crying out and wondering if God's love had ceased, he found hope for his present trouble by remembering: "I will remember the deeds of the LORD; yes, I will remember your wonders of old" (Ps. 77:11). We must *remember*. The God who provided for you yesterday will provide for you tomorrow. The God who carried you through past unemployment or health challenges or deferred dreams will carry you through your current circumstances.

Sometimes we can look back and identify threads of God's faithfulness very clearly, but some of our hurts and trials won't make any sense this side of heaven. We don't always get satisfactory answers or happy endings. So we must remember God's faithfulness to the saints who have walked before us. The God of Noah, the God of Jacob, the God of Joseph, the God of Ruth, the God of David, and the God of Mary *is our God*.

Scripture, in particular the Psalms, also meets us in our suffering by showing us how to lament. The world *is* broken and painful, and we won't find any comfort by having a stiff upper lip and trying to argue otherwise. We find comfort when we admit how devastating our circumstances feel and then go to God as hurting children in need of their Father. He will meet us. He will hold us. And one day, he will wipe every tear from our eyes.

During trials, it is often difficult to stay rooted in Scripture. Though there are times we find them rich and comforting, there are other times that we find them dry. We go to them parched, and rather than quenching us, they just leave us thirstier than before. We cry out to God, but his voice seems mute. Even as we pour over these divinely inspired words, precious verses we've highlighted and underlined and memorized don't always make a mark on our hearts.

We must not give up. Even when our efforts feel futile, God is working. We might be planting seeds in dry soil, but he will bring them to fruition in due season. Keep digging.

God also provides comfort to us through his people. Christians aren't meant to be loners. We are part of one body, and when one member hurts, we all do. And though we can experience the unity and care of the body in many ways, the predominant way we are intended to experience it is in the setting of the local church. As we obey God's instructions to bear one another's burdens and encourage one another, he will comfort our souls.

It's certainly not perfect. Sometimes well-meaning friends say unhelpful things. Sometimes they offer solutions when we really need sympathy. Sometimes they try to fix our problems when they should quietly listen to our lament. But if we press into our church communities—despite the flaws within them—we will experience the grace of God. Just as we welcome people into our happiness, we must let them into our sadness. The command to "rejoice with those who rejoice [and] weep with those who weep" (Rom. 12:15) is a two-way street.

After my first son was born, I lost another child to miscarriage. When the news got out, some well-meaning people said unhelpful and insensitive things, while others rallied around me in ways that demonstrated the loving care of God. They prayed for me and cried with me and reminded me that I wasn't alone in my sorrow. They sent me text messages with Scripture verses, not as quick fixes intended to mend my hurting heart but ones that simply pointed me to behold God, the healer of broken hearts.

The enemy loves to use our pain to isolate us and get us stuck in our own heads, for isolated Christians are far easier to lead astray. He tempts us to withdraw because "nobody understands," pulling us away from the comfort God offers. There is some measure of truth to the statement "nobody understands," because even if we are walking through the same trials, we all process them in different ways. Jesus is the only one who fully knows every nuance of our pain. But God calls his people to bear one another's burdens (Gal. 6:2) and to comfort one another with the comfort we have received (2 Cor.1:3–4). In our unique and individual stories, we experience God in ways we wouldn't have otherwise. So when we are surrounded by people who have walked through similar trials, as well as those who have walked through very different ones, we see more of God. There is profound comfort knowing that the same God who carried one person through the pain of infidelity and another through chronic illness is the one walking with you through whatever adversity you face. In our seasons of difficulty, there is hard-won wisdom and tested comfort to be found in our church communities.

God does not want us to walk alone. His children and his word are extensions of his loving care. "After you have suffered a little while, the God of all grace, who has called you to his eternal glory in Christ, will himself restore, confirm, strengthen, and establish you" (1 Pet. 5:10).

Learn to Kiss the Wave

"I have learned to kiss the wave that strikes me against the Rock of Ages"[26]—I love this quote, because it captures how suffering feels a little bit like drowning sometimes. Waves of trial hit us, and we breathlessly search for something to cling to—a rock— to keep us safe.

The danger comes when we cling to the wrong comforts. If we try to numb our feelings with entertainment or alcohol or food, we find only momentary relief, and it's not long before the ache returns. If we place our hope in relationships or money or medicine, we will be swept away when they inevitably let us down. "For who is God, but the LORD? And who is a rock, except our God?" (Ps. 18:31). The only place our hope can rest securely is in God, because no wave can shake the Rock of Ages. Not cancer. Not abuse. Not infertility. Not unemployment. He is an immovable fortress to those who have suffered betrayal—those broken and bruised by the sins of another. He is a refuge to the one with unmet desires, unwanted diagnoses, and unspeakable loss.

Even when we can't see God's hand in our circumstances, he hasn't left us. Even when we are confused, his promises remain true. Even when we have nothing left to pray but cries of visceral pain, the Spirit intercedes for us. And when distress strikes so hard that death looks like a welcome friend, he will keep us secure.

God is not troubled by raging waves; he rules them.

That is our hope—God is mightier. There is no comfort to be found if we try to minimize our suffering. When someone is drowning, nobody says, "At least the water's warm!" Neither should we tell a grieving mother, "At least you miscarried early," or tell an abuse survivor, "At least you're safe now." While gratitude is undoubtedly a mark of a true Christian, so is lament. We are not called to plaster over pain but to cling to the rock who shelters us through it.

Having joy amidst sorrow testifies to the faithfulness of God. However, we don't get there by gritting our teeth and forcing a smile. We don't just shallowly "look for the bright side of things." Rather, it is in the dark side of things that we discover God's unmatchable worth. We find that he doesn't let go when we have no strength to hold on, and that he remains when everything else is washed away. We find that nothing—no trial or tribulation—can separate us from the love of God in Christ Jesus.[27]

When It Gets Dark

Some of our suffering happens in the confines of our own minds. And though depression, anxiety, panic attacks, and suicidal thoughts can undoubtedly be aggravated by sin, this is *not* always the case. The hormonal changes of having a baby can spark postpartum depression. Trauma can leave lasting imprints on our brain that, when triggered, cause emotional turmoil and spiked cortisol levels. Diseases that attack other parts of our bodies can also attack our minds. Sometimes there's not even a reason we can put our finger on—we just struggle, even if we're growing spiritually.

I'm not an expert, but I imagine that most Christians who wrestle with depression and anxiety disorders also wrestle with shame—*especially* when we have deeply rooted convictions in God's goodness and sovereignty. We want to will our emotions into submission, to force our feelings to match what we believe. But sometimes we can't.

When we have sunk so low, it's tempting to withdraw from community and withhold our struggles. We cannot. God gives grace to the humble, and we must open up to trustworthy brothers and sisters so that they can pray for us, speak truth to us, help shoulder our burdens, and even keep us accountable to seek counseling or medical help. God uses the church to protect the weak, but we must be willing to expose our weaknesses first.

It is also tempting to neglect spiritual disciplines. Knowing that tomorrow may feel overwhelmingly dark, we must devote ourselves to Scripture while we have presence of mind and lift our voices to the Father while we still have words. We do this in faith-filled hope that our labor is not in vain. Sowing today will help us persevere tomorrow.

Learning to endure through a season of severe depression and suicidal ideation was an experience I never would have chosen. It was painful, disorienting, and exhausting. Ever tempted toward "bootstrap faith," I resented my inability to grit my teeth and get over it. But through my weakness, God ministered to me. And through medicine, he helped me.

While agonizing, our mental and physiological battles teach us. We learn to dig into Scripture by faith, despite feeling no immediate impact on our hearts. We learn to pray amidst emotional havoc, trusting that God doesn't care about eloquence and bends his ear toward our incoherent pleas for help. We learn to worship even as we weep for the pain to stop. We learn to open up, even though revealing our struggles is humbling and hard to do. We learn that our efforts to embrace good theology and spiritual disciplines—though crucial—are not enough, and that we *utterly* depend on God to sustain us.

Our struggles are not pointless, a hiccup in God's divine plan. He is using each one of them to conform us into the image of his Son. He will not waste our racing hearts or rolling tears, and even our most desperate cries are sacrifices of worship when offered at his feet.

The Comfort of Heaven

Suffering has a way of clarifying our perspective. When life is going well, we are tempted to grow comfortable with thinking this is all there is. We know it's not true, but functionally we live as if it were. Why long for heaven when earth is so good? So we fill ourselves up on distraction, amusement, and momentary pleasures, muting the inward longing of our hearts.

But in seasons of pain, our desperation for comfort reminds us of how much we long for heaven. It reminds us that this life isn't all there is, and it's certainly not all we want. We live in broken bodies in a sin-ravaged world. We are at war against spiritual forces, worldly influences, and our own sinful hearts. Our bodies and brains have been damaged by the fall. Suffering stirs a holy discontentment as we long for the restoration of all things.

When there are fractures in our relationships, we long to experience complete reconciliation. When there is division in our churches, we long to enjoy eternal unity with our brothers and sisters. When we see news of another mass shooting, another sex abuse scandal, another hate crime, another abortion statistic, we long to live where justice reigns. When we are discouraged over our lack of growth and persistent sin struggles, we long to be free of temptation. When we are tormented by sickness, disability, and disease, we long for new bodies and minds. Ultimately, we long to be with Jesus, worshiping him in the fullness of his glory. Every ounce of suffering we endure can be a reminder of the ultimate healing and joy to come.

So we should never view longings for heaven as the morbid musings of the depressed. Paul said, "For to me to live is Christ, and to die is gain" (Phil. 1:21). We may well face seasons that make us long to die, for in Christ, death *is* gain, but we can persist in hope. As the bride of Christ, our veil has been lifted. But for now, we only see in part. We must walk an aisle paved by both blessing and affliction until we come face-to-face with our Redeemer. Only then will he remove every blemish and wipe every tear from our eyes so that we can finally see his glory clearly. Until then, we groan. Until then, we long. Until then, we hope.

> Blessed is the man who remains steadfast under trial, for when he has stood the test he will receive the crown of life, which God has promised to those who love him. (James 1:12)

Reflection Questions

1. Read James 1:2–4 and Psalm 119:71. Consider a trial you've endured in the past. How did it produce steadfastness? What did you learn about God?

2. How can suffering affect our view of God? How does the truth of God's love, wisdom, and sovereignty help us suffer well?

3. Where is God calling you to repent of ways you have sought comfort by either abusing good gifts (food, relationships, recreation, etc.) or indulging sin (drunkenness, pornography, gossip, materialism, etc.)? What would repentance look like?

4. What anchors of truth can we cling to when we feel rocked by suffering?

5. What does godly lament look like? How does this function in your life?

6. When we ache over our broken world, how does the promise of heaven bring hope?

Recommended Reading

Vaneetha Risner, *The Scars that Have Shaped Me: How God Meets Us in Suffering* (Minneapolis: Desiring God, 2016).

Elisabeth Elliot, *Suffering Is Never for Nothing* (New York: B&H, 2019).

9

Craving Community

"IT IS NOT GOOD that the man should be alone" (Gen. 2:18). Before sinners needed saving or a broken world needed restoring, God asserted that something wasn't right. Who could have expected such an early plot twist? He'd created a beautiful universe, and yet something was missing. Eternally existing as the Trinity, God had always enjoyed relationship as Father, Son, and Spirit. Since Adam was his image bearer, he was made to have relationships too. So God made Eve.

Our longing for family and friendship isn't the result of the fall—it's the result of God's *original* plan. We need community. When we don't have it, we will feel an emptiness, a longing, a craving, one that isn't rooted in discontentment but rooted in our very design.

Believing in the sufficiency of God, it seems counterintuitive to stake the claim that we *need* other relationships too. Yet God has fashioned us this way. Just like he's created us to require oxygen and water and food to live, he's created us to need one another.

When we come to faith in Christ, our reconciled relationship with God binds us even closer together. An almighty King has gathered us as a people and chosen us to proclaim his excellencies among the nations. A heavenly Father has adopted us as his children and brought us into a family of brothers and sisters. Christ, the head, has united us as his body, and we cannot separate from it. Severed limbs rot.

It is not good that man should be alone, and it never was. So God made the church.

The invisible church spans across nations and history and is comprised of all God's people. Someday, we will join voices with people from every tribe and tongue to sing the glories of our Savior. We will listen to the stories of the saints who walked before us and praise God for the perseverance of brothers and sisters who endured persecution. We will celebrate reunions with old friends and have eternity to get to know the rest of God's chosen people. All our earthly divisions will recede, and we will finally—completely—live as one.

We get little glimpses of that reality now. During a missions trip to India, I remember sharing dinner with Christian men and women from India, South Africa, the United States, and the Philippines. We came from different nations, traditions, and churches, yet we all worshiped the same God. It was a sweet taste of heaven. The global church—Christ's very bride—is beautiful to behold.

In this chapter we'll see that God has also called us to something harder, grittier—and just as glorious. He instituted the *local* church so that we can manifest our corporate identity in specific times and places. It is primarily in the context of the local church that we learn to live as one *people*, one *family*, and one *body*. It is primarily in the context of the local church that God generously gives us the fellowship for which we long.

It's a bit messier than that meal I shared in India. It rarely seems like a sweet taste of heaven and can be downright painful at times. But as we live according to our identity in our local church, we will grow in both holiness *and* wholeness. We won't be alone, and it will be very good.

A People

In Western culture, the high regard for autonomy and obsession with individualism has come at a cost: community. This lack of community (coupled with other factors) has contributed to rising loneliness, impacting our physical and mental well-being. In the church, it's impacting our spiritual health too.

When cultural Christianity was the norm, many who grew up in or around church inherited a false assurance of salvation. Mounting concerns over this problem resulted in a new focus on personal relationships with Jesus. This wasn't entirely ill-founded. God loves us as individuals and calls us as individuals to follow him. Going to church doesn't save you. Having Christian parents doesn't save you. Living in the Bible Belt doesn't save you. Jesus does, indeed, require personal allegiance.

However, well-intentioned efforts to emphasize the importance of a personal relationship with God have inadvertently diminished the importance of our corporate relationship. It doesn't end with just "Jesus and me." God has saved us individually to become a *people*: "You are a chosen race, a royal priesthood, a holy nation, a people for his own possession, that you may proclaim the excellencies of him who called you out of darkness into his marvelous light. Once you were not a people, but now you are God's people; once you had not received mercy, but now you have received mercy" (1 Pet. 2:9–10).

When we come to faith in Christ, we obtain citizenship into God's kingdom. We aren't lone rangers; we are indelibly linked to God's people. If we imagine that life is just about "me and Jesus," we won't function as faithful citizens.

God has set apart his church as a holy nation. One that operates with righteousness and justice, where the prosperous share with the poor and the powerful protect the weak. One where individuals work for the common good, more passionate about corporate flourishing than selfish gain. A place where the inhabitants don't only consider their own interests, but "decide never to put a stumbling block" and to "pursue what makes for peace and for mutual upbuilding" (Rom. 14:13, 19). A place overflowing with truth and grace and love.

Surrounding this holy nation, there is a war waging. So while we await the return of our King, we arm ourselves for battle. We watch out for each other and protect one another from the flaming darts of the evil one. Paul urges us to patiently admonish the idle, encourage the fainthearted, and help the weak (1 Thess. 5:14). We carry out the mission together, inviting others to join the kingdom that will not be shaken. When enemies are in our midst—seeking to deceive and dismantle the kingdom—we drive them out. And when the battle seems bleak and our hope wavers, we remind each other that God has already won.

Oh, what a lonely road it would be if Christianity was only about our individual relationships with God! Life is full of trials and tribulations. Jesus warned that we will be hated and scorned for following him. Knowing that we are not alone is profoundly comforting. We aren't the first Christians to suffer for his name, and we won't be the last. We are citizens who work together, soldiers who battle together, and elect exiles who joyfully await a better place.

Together we are called to fight the good fight of faith. Together we are called to follow our King. And since we're still sinners who often fail to live this calling out, together we must repent and forgive as we strive for peace and put bitterness to death.

A Family

We become brothers and sisters the moment God adopts us into his family. There is no hierarchy of worth, no disparaging distinctions (Gal. 3:28–29). And though the roles we play and the gifts we bring to the church vary according to God's good design, we are bound together and equal coheirs with Christ.

This familial language isn't just an analogy. We are *actually* family. Those bought by Christ's blood are even closer than blood. This has massive implications for how we live out community.

As a family, we are called to love one another. It is a simple truth that is profoundly difficult to apply. When conflict arises within the church, it's easy to retreat into our corners, content to build relationships only with those who think and feel and act like us. Our Father isn't tolerant of such an attitude—what loving father would be?

One of the hardest parts of motherhood is when my children mistreat each other. It's painful to watch their partiality, their bickering, their pride, their harshness. Because I love each of them so much, my heart aches when they sin against each other. How much more does it sadden God?

When there is bitterness or anger or slander in the family, we "grieve the Holy Spirit of God," who calls us to "be kind to one another, tenderhearted, forgiving one another" (Eph. 4:30–32). Our Father is not unmoved by our mistreatment of each other, because he loves *each* of us with tender affection. We can't choose to love some brothers and sisters while hating others, because "whoever loves God must also love his brother" (1 John 4:21). As God's children, we are called to reconcile, to cover offenses, and to seek his help when working through our inevitable dysfunction.

Speaking of dysfunction, it is nothing new. Sometimes we romanticize the New Testament church, remembering only its power and none of its problems. There is no denying God's transformative work among the early Christians and the example it sets for us today: they exhibited boldness in persecution, remarkable generosity, and evangelistic fervor. Yet they had plenty of dysfunction too: sexual immorality, divisions, dissensions, false teachers, prejudice, conflict, and lawsuits. This is helpful to remember, because if we conjure an idealized version of the church, we'll be disillusioned when ours inevitably falls short.

Every local church has baggage. Though it's right to be concerned for the holiness, doctrinal purity, and missional faithfulness of our churches, we must extend plenty of grace toward its failures too. God calls us to love the family we *have*, not the better version we imagine. Dietrich Bonhoeffer insightfully wrote:

Every human wish dream that is injected into the Christian community is a hindrance to genuine community and must be banished if genuine community is to survive. He who loves his dream of community more than the Christian community itself becomes a destroyer of the latter, even though his personal intentions may be ever so honest and earnest and sacrificial.[28]

Only through committed love for our brothers and sisters will we resemble our Father's love. If we bail during conflict, if we are slow to forgive, if we are quick to gossip, and if we "bite and devour" one another (Gal. 5:15), how are we any different from the world? Living as brothers and sisters doesn't mean that there is an absence of discord, but that there is a commitment to work through it. After all, that's what helps a family grow closer. Our relationships become deeper and sweeter and stronger the more we bear with one another in love. Treating each other as family is costly, but it brings great comfort too—eternally tied together, we *can't* just give up on each other!

I still attend the church in which I grew up. Along with mutual encouragement and care, there has been hurt and disappointment and conflict. In a very real sense, it feels like my family. When someone I've known for years speaks a hard word of truth, there's an existing foundation that reminds me she is for me. And when someone I've known for years sins against me, it's harder to build walls of bitterness because we share a history of love.

Whether you've been going to the same church for twenty-five years or recently became a member of one, remember: they are your family. Flawed and sinful as we are, we are going to spend eternity together. Let's honor our Father by loving one another now.

A Body

Sometimes I think everyone should be like me. Surely the church would be a better place if people were as passionate about the same doctrines and ministry as I am. This mindset is obviously a gross manifestation of pride, but I am still tempted to let it function.

All temptation is common to man, and this one lures us in several ways. Even if we don't think others should be like *us*, we are tempted to criticize them for being different than *we* think they should be. Our concern is no longer about sin and holiness but about preferences and personalities. We get frustrated when they don't think through doctrine the way we do. We wish they were bolder or quieter about social issues. We are overly critical of pastoral leadership, discontent that our leaders aren't as dynamic and eloquent as our favorite celebrity preachers. We can't understand why fellow church members aren't as committed to the same areas of ministries we are. We assume people have misaligned priorities, when they merely have different priorities from ours. We conflate gifting with godliness, placing unfair expectations on others.

Though our differences sometimes cause friction, they are *good*. By God's design, our churches are comprised of people with different passions and perspectives and personalities for a reason. He has sovereignly bestowed each of us with varied gifts and called us to steward them for our corporate flourishing. Paul wrote, "Now there are varieties of gifts, but the same Spirit; and there are varieties of service, but the same Lord; and there are varieties of activities, but it is the same God who empowers them all in everyone. To each is given the manifestation of the Spirit *for the common good*" (1 Cor. 12:4–7).

By embracing our different functions, the whole body grows healthier. We were never supposed to be the same, "for as in one body we have many members, and the members do not all have the same function, so we, though many, are one body in Christ, and individually members one of another" (Rom. 12:4–5).

We are not born again as clones. To think we are called to sameness is just as ridiculous as believing a body should be comprised of only hands or eyes or toes. It would never survive! The body of Christ cannot be healthy apart from our different functions. God has designed you and me with specific abilities to serve particular purposes. Are we exercising them? Are we lying dormant, as if we have no role in the body, or are we living for ourselves, as if we were disconnected from the body? When we don't faithfully serve our function, we are impairing the body of Christ.

Our differences also contribute to our joint growth in holiness. God has given us strengths to help others in their weaknesses (and vice versa). I tend to be thoughtful, bold, and passionate in my convictions. This is an evidence of God's work in my life. I have, however, coinciding weaknesses: I can be arrogant, self-righteous, and harsh. God has used people like my friend Katie to help me grow in humility and gentleness. Katie and I will always have different personalities, but as we function together in our local body, we can help each other walk in submission to Christ, our head.

Embracing differences never means tolerating sin—the body of Christ is called to be holy. If Katie were to correct me for speaking harshly, I shouldn't say, "Well, Katie, we're just different. That's how I express 'passion' sometimes." Rather, I should value how God is using her, as one member of the body, to help me, as another member of the body, to fight sin.

Just as sickness impacts the whole body, ungodliness does too—we are deeply vested in one another's spiritual health.

This is why we so desperately *need* community with those different from us. We can't just pursue relationships with Christians who serve similar functions. Hands and arms might get along better, but they won't be going anywhere without the feet.

A Protection

Despite our innate desire for community, we still recoil against it. Sometimes we don't want the accountability of those who know us best. We don't want others involved in our lives and crave the false freedom of autonomy. Relationships entail responsibilities—particularly for Christians—and sometimes we just want to be free of them.

Removing ourselves from community is dangerous. This is why Scripture warns, "Whoever isolates himself seeks his own desire; he breaks out against all sound judgment" (Prov. 18:1). In isolation we get trapped in the echo chamber of our own minds. There, it's much easier to be enticed by sin and fall prey to deception. There, it's much easier to plunge into despair and feel overcome by condemnation.

Christian community offers protection. God has ordained pastoral shepherds to watch over our souls (Heb. 13:17) and to instruct us in sound doctrine (Titus 1:9). He has called brothers and sisters to bring us back from wandering (James 5:19–20) and to gently restore us when we are caught in transgression (Gal. 6:1).

We have an enemy who is waging war on our souls. Even though we've been won to Christ, this enemy stops at nothing to encumber our faith. Left to ourselves, we'll be tempted to drift into false teaching and ungodly living. Left to ourselves, sin will start sparkling, and we'll devise ways to justify it. And once we take the bait, we'll be caught by the hook—we need others to help us get loose.

As we stumble and sin, the enemy relentlessly accuses us. He wants us to give up, which is easy to do if we feel cornered and isolated. He will seek to crush our spirits with condemnation and make us question whether God's forgiveness still stands. When we feel condemned, we need others to remind us that God's grace covers our guilt. When we feel broken, we need others to remind us of the one who was broken for us so that we could be made whole.

Isolation also compounds our temptation to grow discouraged. We must consider "how to stir up one another to love and good works, *not neglecting to meet together*, as is the habit of some, but *encouraging one another*, and all the more as you see the Day drawing near" (Heb. 10:24–25).

The world is full of hollow cheerleaders telling us that our sin isn't that bad (everyone messes up!) and to stay positive when life gets hard (everything happens for a reason!) This shallow encouragement may keep us afloat for a little while, but it offers no real protection for our souls.

Sin is serious. Life is hard. So our only real encouragement is God's unchanging word, and who can better remind us of that than others who know it? We'll likely have our "Job moments," when the friends who were supposed to encourage us add to our burden instead (and we'll likely be guilty of the same). Still, we must press on, trusting God to faithfully work through others to protect and minister to us. After all, even Job's fallen companions spent an entire week lamenting with him before saying a word. Who knows how God used their initial presence to keep him from abandoning hope?

Marked by Love

As we increasingly live out true community, something remarkable happens. Not only do we *individually* enjoy the blessing of Christian love; we also *collectively* demonstrate the transforming effect of the gospel to the world. As Jesus said, "By this all people will know that you are my disciples, if you have love for one another" (John 13:35).

We are a ragtag group of disciples with all sorts of differences, and the only explanation for our love is the work of Jesus Christ. He is the one who renews our hearts and enables us to practice the love defined in 1 Corinthians 13. By his grace, we can be patient and kind to those unlike us; we won't envy each others' circumstances or boast in our own; we won't be arrogant in our opinions or rude in our actions; we will serve instead of insisting on our own way; we will put to death irritation and resentment; we won't rejoice in wrongdoing, but we will rejoice with the truth (13:4–6). By his grace, our love can bear all things, believe all things, hope all things, and endure all things (13:7). What a testimony!

Only Jesus can turn enemies into family. Only Jesus can bring lasting reconciliation among sinners. Only Jesus can fully unify where there is deep division. Only Jesus can enable hearts to love well despite dysfunction. That shows something to others. It shows that we are his.

> The more genuine and the deeper our community becomes, the more will everything else between us recede, the more clearly and purely will Jesus Christ and his work become the one and only thing that is vital between us.[29]

Discussion Questions:

1. Do you see the importance of the local church? Why or why not?

2. What are some ways that God has used the local church to strengthen your faith?

3. Read 1 Corinthians 12:4–7. How has God gifted you? How can you steward those gifts for the good of the church?

4. Read Ephesians 4:2–3. How are humility, gentleness, patience, and forbearance functioning in your life right now? How can you pursue unity among fellow Christians? Why is this commitment so important?

5. Consider how much Christ loves the church—it is the bride for which he died. How can you cultivate a similar love, especially when confronted by its flaws?

6. Read 1 John 4:7–8. Why is love for one another an essential evidence of being God's children?

Recommended Reading

Dietrich Bonhoeffer, *Life Together: The Classic Exploration of Christian Community* (New York: HarperOne, 2009).

Megan Hill, *A Place to Belong: Learning to Love the Local Church* (Wheaton, IL: Crossway, 2020).

10

Craving Mission

"OH MY GOODNESS, you *have* to try this!" Anytime I taste something particularly mind-blowing, I offer a bite to my husband and watch with eager anticipation for his reaction. We do this with all sorts of things. When we're diehard fans of a TV show, we try to convince others to watch it. When we return from an amazing vacation, we encourage others to visit the same place. When we hike a scenic mountain, we post pictures on social media so that others can see its beauty. We're ardent evangelists when it comes to our favorite restaurants, movies, and products. The more we enjoy something, the more we want others to experience it too.

But sometimes there's a disconnect when it comes to God. Though we truly love him, we don't always live to make him known. So God creates a holy restlessness in our souls—a longing for something more. We can't always identify why, and we're tempted to respond by chasing purpose in our jobs or our roles or our ambitions. However good those things might be, if we view them as ultimate—our chief end in life—we will be left disappointed when none of them manages to settle our restlessness.

Don't be discouraged. God stirs our hearts for a reason. Our innate craving for purpose is satisfied by living for *his* mission, *his* kingdom, and *his* glory. Though he doesn't need us, he graciously invites us into the work of making his name known.

Our relationship with God is meant to impact our homes, workplaces, and communities for his glory. As we behold his magnificence, we should want others to see it. As we experience his love, grace, and comfort, we should want others to receive it. As we are anchored in his truth, we should want others to learn it. There is abundant blessing in being called children of God, and sharing that hope compounds our joy. If the chief end of man is to glorify God and enjoy him forever,[30] we should have a burgeoning desire for *others* to enjoy and glorify God too.

It can't just end with us.

God has given us a mission. The good news is too good to keep to ourselves. In this final chapter, we will consider how God calls us to bear witness to the gospel in both word and deed. When this is our mission, it will transform *everything* we do.

The Gospel Proclaimed

Our world is fraught with need. From the moment sin entered, suffering followed. The hungry need food, the enslaved need freedom, the orphaned need family, the sick need healing, the oppressed need justice. War-ravaged countries need peace, and brutalized communities need protection. The whole earth aches for deliverance; it yearns for restoration from brokenness.

As urgent as those needs are, there is an even greater one—reconciliation with God. In red states and blue states, among the rich and poor, across ethnic lines and ages, there is a common problem: people are lost. We are, by nature, children of wrath, sinners who are separated from God (Eph. 2:3). Whatever the differences between us, sin is our greatest problem, salvation is our greatest need, and sharing the gospel is our greatest call.

Just like the disciples he was speaking to, we have been commissioned and empowered by Jesus to spread the hope of the gospel: "All authority in heaven and on earth has been given to me. Go therefore and make disciples of all nations, baptizing them in the name of the Father and of the Son and of the Holy Spirit, teaching them to observe all that I have commanded you" (Matt. 28:18–20). Gospel proclamation and discipleship aren't just for pastors and preachers or for the eloquent and seminary-educated. The whole church is entrusted with this mission, and each of us plays an integral part. God worked through religious experts like Paul *and* through gruff fishermen like Peter. His fame spread through successful businesswomen like Lydia and through little children. The same is true today. Though God sometimes builds his kingdom through brilliant apologists and evangelists, he doesn't depend on them. He can work through you and me too.

So be encouraged. The power of the gospel doesn't rest in our persuasiveness; it rests in the authority of the one who sends us and in the gospel message itself (1 Cor. 1:18).

In his sovereignty, God—"who desires all people to be saved and to come to the knowledge of the truth" (1 Tim. 2:4)—has placed us in our families and neighborhoods and workplaces for a purpose. We are sent to spread the good news of Jesus Christ, who came to rescue sinners. Whether we live in the suburbs or the projects, we are called to spread this message. When we go to work or grad school or tuck our children into bed, we are called to spread this message. Spiritual need exists everywhere, so our mission does too.

The gospel is our anthem until our dying breath. There is nothing more beautiful, worthy, and hope-giving to offer a broken, needy, and sin-ravaged world.

While our actions are an intrinsic and irreplaceable aspect of our witness to others, preaching the gospel requires words. We are not preaching the gospel with our lives if we are not also preaching the gospel with our lips. Generosity, social activism, and neighborly kindness alone cannot show people that they are separated from God and in need of a savior. Good works alone cannot impart the good news that Christ died to redeem sinners. Words must be spoken or else the gospel will not be spread. "For everyone who calls on the name of the Lord will be saved. How then will they call on him in whom they have not believed? And how are they to believe in him of whom they have never heard? And how are they to hear without someone preaching?" (Rom. 10:13–14).

To embrace this mission, it's important that we prepare for rejection. Followers of Christ need soft hearts and thick skin. We must ache with compassion for the unbeliever, adamantly desiring their reconciliation with God; we must graciously bear insult and mistreatment, joyfully sharing in the sufferings of Christ. And though preaching the gospel to a world that rejects it is often disheartening, we have every reason to hope:

We should have confidence because we know the mission will not fail. We may fail in our faithfulness, but God will not fail in his mission. Christ will have the nations for his inheritance. Frantic speculation and guilt are weak motivators compared with the truth of God's unstoppable plan to rescue every child for whom Christ died. Christ will not lose any of those whom the Father has given him, and God has chosen us—in countless local churches—as agents of his gospel triumph.[31]

The Gospel Demonstrated

As God's beloved children, we are called to be imitators of him. It is vital to faithful mission. After all, if we *preach* what is true about God without *representing* what is true about God, why would anyone listen to us?

God cares about human suffering. He carefully knits every human being into existence and treasures every unborn child (Ps. 139:13–14). He is a father to the fatherless and a protector of widows (Ps. 68:5). He watches over the sojourner—to use modern terms, the immigrant, migrant, asylum seeker, and refugee (Ps. 146:9). He hears the cry of the poor (Ps. 102:17), and his fury rises at their abuse (Prov. 17:5). His compassion stretches to those who face hunger and persecution and to those degraded because of their disability or ethnicity (Ps. 146:7–8).

And we are called to share his heart.

In the Old Testament, the Israelites were commanded to live differently from the surrounding culture, to reflect the nature of God and the ethics of his kingdom. They were specifically instructed to care for the poor, the fatherless, the widow, and the sojourner—to protect them from injustice, to share their harvest and allot a portion of tithe for their provision, and to include them in feasts and celebrations as members of the community.

Though the modern church isn't called to specific Israelite practices like gleaning or celebrating the year of jubilee, it's important to understand that the moral responsibility to demonstrate mercy and justice was *not* uniquely assigned to the Israelites.

God described Job as "a blameless and upright man, who fears God and turns away from evil" (Job 1:8), and a *primary* aspect of Job's righteousness was how he cared for the needy. When Job's friends claimed that his suffering was the result of sin, Job defended himself in this way:

> If I have withheld anything that the poor desired, or have caused the eyes of the widow to fail, or have eaten my morsel alone, and the fatherless has not eaten of it (for from my youth the fatherless grew up with me as with a father, and from my mother's womb I guided the widow), if I have seen anyone perish for lack of clothing, or the needy without covering, if his body has not blessed me, and if he was not warmed with the fleece of my sheep, if I have raised my hand against the fatherless, because I saw my help in the gate, then let my shoulder blade fall from my shoulder, and let my arm be broken from its socket. (Job 31:16–22)

Job was so appalled at the thought of neglecting the vulnerable that he dramatically invited physical mutilation if he was found guilty of doing so. As a righteous man, passivity wasn't an option.

Rather than following Job's example, we are tempted to do the reverse and justify ourselves for our lack of mercy and justice. Even though we label such practices as good, we consider them in the realm of extracurricular Christian activity.

But in the same way we shouldn't view sexual purity or honesty as optional to Christian obedience, we shouldn't consider these good works optional either. Such actions are essential fruits of righteousness for those who follow God: "He has told you, O man, what is good; and what does the LORD *require* of you but to do justice, and to love kindness, and to walk humbly with your God?" (Mic. 6:8).

Mercy and justice aren't just tenets to believe; they are deeds to do. Pay attention to the actions italicized in the following two passages:

> *Give* justice to the weak and the fatherless;
>   *maintain* the right of the afflicted and the destitute.
> *Rescue* the weak and the needy;
>   *deliver* them from the hand of the wicked. (Ps. 82:3–4)

> *Learn* to do good;
> *seek* justice,
>   *correct* oppression;
> *bring* justice to the fatherless,
>   *plead* the widow's cause. (Isa. 1:17)

Scripture simply hasn't given us the option to sit on the sidelines. When we discern oppression, it's so that we can pursue justice. When we discern the needs of the vulnerable, it's so that we can respond in some way. If our action—or inaction—robs people of mercy and justice, we are dishonoring God and devaluing his image bearers.

In the New Testament, Jesus also emphasizes this crucial aspect of faith. In a sobering account of the final judgment, he depicts how acts of mercy such as feeding the hungry, welcoming the stranger, and clothing the naked will distinguish between those who are his people and those who aren't (Matt. 25:31–46). This distinction doesn't mean that our works earn our place in the kingdom. Rather, they show that the King already reigns over our hearts.

When the gospel transforms us, it changes how we treat others. God cares—intensely—for those who suffer. If we are born of him, we will too.

Jesus did more than provide us with instructions and warnings. He *demonstrated* consistent compassion toward the needy. He showed tenderness to women, children, and the disabled—those marginalized by society and deemed "less than." He healed the sick, cast out demons, touched the unclean, and fed the hungry. These miracles were unquestionably intended to point to his divinity, but they were also meant to point to his *heart*. Jesus doesn't just have power to multiply bread and fish; he has compassion for the hungry. He doesn't just have power to heal; he has compassion for the hurting.

To be truly gospel centered, we must be gospel transformed. We must preach the good news *and* be devoted to good works for the glory of his name. This devotion to good works starts within the body of Christ and extends outward. In our zeal for the mission, we must remember what we learned in the previous chapter: love expressed *in* the church is essential to our witness. Paul emphasized this priority: "So then, as we have opportunity, let us do good to everyone, and *especially* to those who are of the household of faith" (Gal. 6:10). As we seek to care for people in our communities and around the world, may we never neglect the needs within our own churches.

God has established the church as the light of the world, and we must let our light shine before others so that they may see our good works and give glory to our Father in heaven (Matt. 5:14–16). Through our deeds, we are called to demonstrate the generous, humble, and impartial love of God in the gospel.

Generosity: Demonstrating the Generous Love of God in the Gospel

God is our provider, and all that we have belongs to him. We are stewards, entrusted to use everything we have—be it poverty or wealth—for his glory and our neighbor's good.

Biblical generosity is not mere charity; it is a demonstration of the gospel. Jesus set aside a crown of glory to wear a crown of thorns. So great was his love and compassion that he sacrificed his very life to save us. The only reason we know the riches of God's grace is his generous love. "For you know the grace of our Lord Jesus Christ, that though he was rich, yet for your sake he became poor, so that you by his poverty might become rich" (2 Cor. 8:9).

When we give to build the church, the body that exists to breathe good news, others will learn how Jesus gave his life for them. The local church is central to the mission of God, vital for our individual discipleship and corporate witness, which makes generosity toward our churches crucial to advancing the mission.

We are also called to give generously to the poor, remembering that we, ourselves, were once spiritually impoverished. Love and generosity are inextricably linked—the more we grasp God's love for us, the more generous we become to those in need. So entwined is the fruit of generosity to our salvation that a lack of generosity indicates that our faith might be dead:

> What good is it, my brothers, if someone says he has faith but does not have works? Can that faith save him? If a brother or sister is poorly clothed and lacking in daily food, and one of you says to them, "Go in peace, be warmed and filled," without giving them the things needed for the body, what good is that? So also faith by itself, if it does not have works, is dead. (James 2:14–17)

Right now, there are little children dying of preventable diseases because they don't have access to medical care. There are refugees living in tents, mourning the loss of their homeland and not welcome in their new one. There are people with disabilities begging on the streets because their culture called them cursed and robbed them of the chance to learn and grow and thrive. There are men and women who work sunrise to sundown and get paid only two dollars a day.

Jesus said that the poor will always be with us, so we can't expect to eradicate all these problems. But, oh, may our hearts be moved with compassion and compelled to alleviate the suffering we can! May we faithfully and generously and strategically give to people and causes and places that provide holistic care. May we empty ourselves for the sake of the poor, as Christ emptied himself for us.

But how? It feels overwhelming to start. First, we must remember that we aren't all-powerful rescuers; we are just one part of the body, called to faithfully steward whatever God has entrusted to us. Then it's helpful to consider which needs capture our attention. Does your heart burn for orphans or a certain people group unreached by the gospel? If so, God might be calling you to give to a ministry that serves them. Maybe there is a crisis pregnancy center in your town or a counseling service for women who've suffered domestic violence. Maybe you know specific families struggling to make ends meet, and there are tangible ways you can help them. God draws us to different needs on purpose so that *collectively*, we can express his care in more ways than we ever could alone.

When we part with our earthly treasures in order to be generous, we testify to the greater worth of Christ. Everything here is passing away, so we can joyfully give to a kingdom that won't.

Service: Demonstrating the Humble Love of God in the Gospel

Jesus came not to be served but to serve (Matt. 20:28). This truth is so familiar that it often fails to astound us. But it should. The maker and sustainer of all creation came to serve. The ruler of the heavens and the earth came to serve. The King to whom the angels cry, "Holy, holy, holy!" came to serve. Someday we will bow at the feet of the one who washed ours first.

If our glorious God so humbled himself, how much more should we?

We are so prone to pride—to help those who can help us back, treating people as commodities who exist for our benefit. Or we do good deeds in an attempt to feel better about ourselves. Even our service is stained with sin.

True service—humble, loving, sacrificial service—isn't concerned with self at all. We won't seek earthly affirmation or reward because Christ is already our reward, and we just want to show others what he is like. So we tend to the needy, spend time with the lonely, lift up the downtrodden, and speak for the voiceless *because our Savior cares for them.*

Humble servants come alongside the suffering. Rather than considering ourselves above them, we identify with them. Jesus didn't just dole out good deeds from on high. He walked among us. He got close. He drew little children into his lap. He tenderly reached out and touched the leper, even though he could have healed him with a word (Matt. 8:2–3).

Jesus doesn't serve from a distance. His compassion compels him to come close. Unlike us, he'd never wrinkle his nose at the stench of an alcoholic's breath; he'd drape an arm around him and invite him to share the burdens of his heart. He'd never recoil from touching someone's grimy clothes; he'd offer to clean them and share his own shirt in the meantime.

The Israelites had expected the promised Messiah to come as a powerful ruler. Someone who would legislate change and force all wrongs to be made right. But instead of coming in power, Christ emptied himself of it. Even though he was holy and set apart, he humbly chose to identify with us. He laid aside his glory to serve.

As followers of Christ, we are called to live as humble servants. We are called to pour ourselves out to replenish others, to serve with humility just as Christ did, and to leverage any power or privilege we have for the good of the vulnerable. That might mean grocery shopping for an elderly neighbor or babysitting for a single mom or crocheting scarves for the homeless or organizing a food drive or tutoring underprivileged students. There are always ways for us to use our time and talents to serve others. And the more our motivations are rooted in love for Jesus and gratitude for what he's done, the more joy we'll experience as we follow in his steps.

Befriend: Demonstrating the Impartial Love of God in the Gospel

Jesus didn't just come for the Israelites or the religious elite. He didn't just come for the popular or the powerful. He came to save *any* who call upon him for mercy.

We struggle with reflecting this sort of love. We are tempted to love those who love us back (just like the world). We are tempted to show preference to those in high standing (just like the world). We are tempted to stay in our comfort zones, only reaching out to those who share our social, educational, or ethnic backgrounds (just like the world).

The mission of Christ confronts this tendency. Christians are called to befriend the marginalized and mistreated. There is no room for tribalism or nationalism or classism in the kingdom. We were *all* outcasts—strangers of God until he called us friends— so we must reach out to the outcast and make them our friends.

The beauty of the church is our level standing before God. There aren't haves and have-nots. God doesn't play favorites, and he shows no partiality. Those whom the world lifts high are humbled, remembering their need for Christ. Those whom the world disparages are lifted up, remembering their glory in Christ.

So the church must seek to reflect this truth now. We must look around and befriend those unlike us, with a particular concern for the overlooked and forgotten. This might entail spending time with the widow down the street or the next-door neighbor who has special needs. For me, it has meant befriending refugees who resettled in my area. For *all* of us, it means extending hospitality (Heb. 13:2). Defined biblically, hospitality isn't just about hosting dinner parties for friends and family. It's about reaching out and loving strangers.[32]

There is nothing flashy about befriending people. It doesn't feel quite as exciting as launching a nonprofit or leading a conference or traveling overseas as a missionary. But the mission isn't supposed to be flashy. Usually it is comprised of small and intentional choices, practiced over a long period of time. Usually the fruit is slow and grows with little fanfare.

And even when God chooses to work in big ways, he uses ordinary faithfulness to do so. My best friend is a foster mom. After years of building relationships with children and families involved in foster care, God revealed new ways she could use her talents to serve them. Now she directs a nonprofit that serves hundreds of foster families. If she had skipped the humble beginnings of building relationships, the nonprofit would never have been born in the first place.

If we focus too broadly, the vast needs of a suffering world will leave us overwhelmed. Being overwhelmed leads to discouragement, discouragement leads to hopelessness, and hopelessness leads to inaction. But if we faithfully focus on caring for the *one*, God will reveal other ways he's equipped us for his mission too. You can't welcome every child who needs a home, but maybe you can become a foster parent to one. I can't visit every refugee who lives nearby, but I can get to know a few.

Time Is Running Out

The imminence of our eternal home gives us so much to look forward to. Just think—we have all eternity to behold the majesty of God. We have all eternity to love and be loved by him. We have all eternity to live in community with our brothers and sisters. We have all eternity to enjoy God's gifts of beauty and work and creativity and fun.

Conversely, the time allotted for some endeavors is running out. God's work here isn't done. He is still seeking and saving the lost. He is still restoring and redeeming the broken. And he has invited us to join in his labor.

This changes how we dream and live and make decisions. It gives us eyes to see what sin has broken so that we can use the tools God has given us to participate in healing it. It loosens the grasp of materialism and allows us to live more generously. It gives us the spiritual stamina necessary to endure rejection without becoming embittered.

Awaiting eternity fills us with a hopeful urgency. We have only from now until death to spread the gospel to the lost, to minister to the needs of the poor, and to seek justice for the oppressed. When it comes to the task of mercy-filled mission, our days are numbered—we must use them well!

If you live gladly to make others glad in God, your life will be hard, your risks will be high, and your joy will be full.[33]

Discussion Questions

1. What is the biggest stumbling block for you when it comes to sharing the gospel? How does trusting the gospel's inherent

power (rather than your education, eloquence, or disposition) encourage you?

2. Read 1 John 3:16–18. Why are deeds of mercy so essential to our gospel witness?

3. Read Luke 12:32–34. How can you grow as a generous steward of your money and possessions?

4. Where has God positioned you to serve others, particularly the spiritually lost or physically vulnerable? How can you grow in servanthood?

5. Read Luke 14:12–14. Whom might God be calling you to befriend? How will you pursue them?

6. How can a sense of restlessness, coupled with an eternal perspective, drive you to live on mission?

Recommended Reading

Elliot Clark, *Evangelism as Exiles: Life on Mission as Strangers in Our Own Land* (Austin, TX: The Gospel Coaltion, 2019).

Timothy Keller, *Ministries of Mercy: The Call of the Jericho Road* (Phillipsburg, NJ: P&R, 2015).

Conclusion

I TALK ABOUT FOOD the way some people talk about sports. I can't help but grow animated with excitement when I describe the potato poori I had in India or the tiramisu I had in Italy or the kobbah my Syrian friend makes. I love tasting the different elements and flavors of Mexican, Italian, Thai, Indian, Chinese, and Middle Eastern cuisine. And once I've tried something particularly delicious, I live in eager expectation of eating it again.

Because I've had the opportunity to taste such delicious dishes, my expectations for good food have risen over time. The positive side of this is that it's motivated me to become a better cook (much to my family's delight). The negative side is that I have to fight the impulse to be a critical and ungrateful food snob.

Hunger for God, however, is *always* a good thing. While physical hunger is roused by daily appetite or sinful gluttony or the need for survival—and can be settled with the right blend of calories, regardless of how good it tastes—spiritual hunger is intended to make us feast. It should make "food snobs" out of us all.

God doesn't want us to be satisfied with moderate portions of him. He isn't interested in placating us with just enough to be appeased. In love, he stirs our spiritual hunger over and over so that we continually return to him to be filled. He gives us hungry hearts so that he can abundantly gratify them. Our longings were never meant to be stifled, "for he satisfies the longing soul, and the hungry soul he fills with good things" (Ps. 107:9).

Each time our hunger for hope or joy or peace or purpose sends us to God, we will taste and see that he is good. He is always better than we anticipated, always better than we remembered. And though it seems a paradox, we will find that the more he fills us, the more we want him. True satisfaction in God leads to an ever-increasing longing for him, and that longing won't leave us disappointed. He is—and eternally will be—more than enough.

> Whom have I in heaven but you?
>   And there is nothing on earth that I desire besides you.
> My flesh and my heart may fail,
>   but God is the strength of my heart and my portion forever.
>   (Ps. 73:25–26)

Acknowledgments

GOD HAS BEEN exceedingly gracious to me, and I am so grateful for the many people he's placed in my life to help shape this book. Andrew, thank you for your unwavering support, encouragement, and willingness to read *every* draft. You are my best friend, and I love being married to you. Isaac, Reed, and Tulasi, thank you for your patience whenever my "almost done" turned into much longer. You bring me so much joy, and I love being your mom.

Dad and Jeff, thank you for your help and theological insight—you are my favorite pastors. Mom, thank you for encouraging and editing my work ever since kindergarten—once a homeschool mom, always a homeschool mom. My sisters, thank you for cheering me on, reading messy drafts, and caring for my heart through this process. Emily and Mom D, thank you for babysitting and giving me extended time to write. Jamie, thank you for being the kind of friend who's willing to give constructive criticism, and then brings over chocolate and cheese to celebrate the news of my book being published.

Megan Hill and Melissa Kruger, thank you for the invaluable feedback you provided to make this a better book. Dave DeWit, thank you for catching the vision and helping me sharpen my ideas. Lydia Brownback, thank you for advocating for this project at the beginning and polishing it at the end. And to the rest of the team at Crossway, thank you for all your work behind the scenes to get this book into print.

Notes

1. A. W. Tozer, *The Knowledge of the Holy* (New York: HarperCollins, 1961), 18.
2. Victor Kiprop, "How Many Animals Are There in the World?," *World Atlas*, March 20, 2018, https://www.worldatlas.com/.
3. Jerry Bridges, *The Joy of Fearing God* (Colorado Springs, CO: Waterbrook, 1997), 59.
4. Isaac Watts, "The Heavens Declare Thy Glory, Lord," 1719.
5. Quoted in Tozer, *Knowledge of the Holy*, 14.
6. *Life Is Beautiful*, directed by Roberto Benigni (Los Angeles: Miramax, 1997).
7. Tozer, *Knowledge of the Holy*, 98.
8. Jerry Bridges, *Respectable Sins: Confronting the Sins We Tolerate* (Colorado Springs, CO: NavPress, 2007).
9. R. C. Sproul, *The Holiness of God* (Wheaton, IL: Tyndale, 1985), 116.
10. Jerry Bridges, *The Discipline of Grace: God's Role and Our Role in the Pursuit of Holiness* (Colorado Springs, CO: NavPress, 1994), 18.
11. Tozer, *Knowledge of the Holy*, 20.
12. Jackie Hill Perry, *Gay Girl, Good God: The Story of Who I Was, and Who God Has Always Been* (Nashville, TN: B&H, 2018), 180.
13. Jen Wilkin, *In His Image: 10 Ways God Calls Us to Reflect His Character* (Wheaton, IL: Crossway, 2018), 130.
14. J. I. Packer, *Concise Theology: A Guide to Historic Christian Beliefs* (Carol Stream, IL: Tyndale, 1993), 170.
15. *The Lord of the Rings: The Two Towers*, directed by Peter Jackson (Burbank, CA: New Line Cinema, 2002).
16. Bridges, *Discipline of Grace*, 132.

17. Charitie Lees Smith, "Before the Throne of God Above," 1863.

18. Charles H. Spurgeon, *Following Christ: Losing Your Life for His Sake*, Kindle ed. (Abbotsford, WI: Aneko Press, 2019), 137.

19. Kathleen Davis, "What to Know about Sleep Deprivation," *Medical News Today*, July 23, 2020, https://www.medicalnewstoday.com/.

20. Cited in Randy Alcorn, *Happiness* (Carol Stream, IL: Tyndale, 2015), 5.

21. Alcorn, *Happiness*, ix.

22. Melanie Greenberg, "How Gratitude Leads to a Happier Life," *Psychology Today*, November 22, 2015, https://www.psychologytoday.com/.

23. Charles Spurgeon, *Morning and Evening* (New Kensington, PA: Whitaker, 1997), 21.

24. *Chariots of Fire*, directed by Hugh Hudson (Los Angeles: 20th Century Fox, 1981).

25. Charles Spurgeon, quoted in Alcorn, *Happiness*, 87.

26. Quote attributed to Charles Spurgeon.

27. Portions of this chapter first appeared in Amy DiMarcangelo, "Despair Cannot Drown Us, God Is Greater," *Equipped for Mercy* website, June 24, 2019, https://equippedformercy.com.

28. Dietrich Bonhoeffer, *Life Together: The Classic Exploration of Christian Community*, trans. John W. Doberstein (New York: HarperCollins, 1954), 27.

29. Bonhoeffer, *Life Together*, 26.

30. Westminster Shorter Catechism, in *The Confession of Faith Together with the Larger Catechism and the Shorter Catechism with Scripture Proofs*, 3rd ed. (Lawrenceville, GA: Christian Education & Publications, 1990), Q&A 1.

31. Andy Johnson, *Missions: How the Local Church Goes Global* (Wheaton, IL: Crossway, 2017), 120.

32. The Greek word for *hospitality* is *philoxenia*, which means "the love of strangers."

33. John Piper, *Don't Waste Your Life* (Wheaton, IL: Crossway, 2007), 10.

General Index

Scripture Index

THE GOSPEL COALITION

The Gospel Coalition (TGC) supports the church in making disciples of all nations, by providing gospel-centered resources that are trusted and timely, winsome and wise.

Guided by a Council of more than 40 pastors in the Reformed tradition, TGC seeks to advance gospel-centered ministry for the next generation by producing content (including articles, podcasts, videos, courses, and books) and convening leaders (including conferences, virtual events, training, and regional chapters).

In all of this we want to help Christians around the world better grasp the gospel of Jesus Christ and apply it to all of life in the 21st century. We want to offer biblical truth in an era of great confusion. We want to offer gospel-centered hope for the searching.

Through its women's initiatives, The Gospel Coalition aims to support the growth of women in faithfully studying and sharing the Scriptures; in actively loving and serving the church; and in spreading the gospel of Jesus Christ in all their callings.

Join us by visiting TGC.org so you can be equipped to love God with all your heart, soul, mind, and strength, and to love your neighbor as yourself.

TGC.org

Also Available from
the Gospel Coalition

For more information, visit **crossway.org**.